T0329999

ANTI-CRISIS

ANTI-CRISIS

JANET ROITMAN

DUKE UNIVERSITY PRESS   DURHAM AND LONDON   2014

Printed in the United States of America on acid-free paper ∞
Typeset in Scala and Orator by Tseng Information Systems, Inc.

Library of Congress Cataloging-in-Publication Data
Roitman, Janet L. (Janet Lee)
Anti-crisis / Janet Roitman.
pages cm
Includes bibliographical references and index.
ISBN 978-0-8223-5512-0 (cloth : alk. paper)
ISBN 978-0-8223-5527-4 (pbk. : alk. paper)
1. Crises (Philosophy)
2. Crisis (The English word)
3. History, Modern—21st century. I. Title.
B105.C75R65 2013
302′.17—dc23   2013024847

Permission for lyrics to epigraph on page vii
"Make It with You"
Written by: David Gates
© 1970 Sony/ATV Music Publishing LLC. All rights administered
by Sony/ATV Music Publishing LLC, 8 Music Square West,
Nashville, TN 37203. All rights reserved. Used by permission.

DUKE UNIVERSITY PRESS GRATEFULLY ACKNOWLEDGES
THE SUPPORT OF THE NEW SCHOOL, WHICH PROVIDED
FUNDS TOWARD THE PUBLICATION OF THIS BOOK.

FOR LEONORE AND HARRY ROITMAN

Dreams, they're for those who sleep . . .
—BREAD, "Make It with You"

That, perhaps, was the chief miracle about it.
Here was a woman about the year 1800 writing
without hate, without bitterness, without fear,
without protest, without preaching.
—VIRGINIA WOOLF, *A Room of One's Own* (1929)

CONTENTS

xi   Acknowledgments

1   INTRODUCTION   What Is at Stake?

15   CHAPTER 1   Crisis Demands
JUDGMENT DAY
THE MORAL DEMAND
THE TEST

41   CHAPTER 2   Crisis Narratives
BUBBLES
HOUSES
FINANCE
SUBJECTS

71   CHAPTER 3   Crisis: Refrain!
NONCRISIS NARRATION
THE CRISIS THAT DOES NOT OBTAIN

91   CONCLUSION   Dreams

97   Notes

133   References

153   Index

ACKNOWLEDGMENTS

Many people helped me through crisis. Indeed, I surely would have given up this project and left my mind in crisis had it not been for Martha Poon, Ann Stoler, Mary Murrell, and Paul Rabinow, each of whom sustained and challenged this project in specific ways. Martha Poon, Ann Stoler, and Mary Murrell passed along every crisis text they found. Martha Poon helped me to keep my mind to materiality with regard to a project that seemed lost in idealism. She read myriad drafts, exchanged countless e-mails, debated over drinks, and helped me to see how this project is relevant to many practical endeavors in academe and beyond. Her comments and edits on chapters 2 and 3 are especially appreciated; but, overall, this book benefits enormously from Martha's own research; it clearly would not have been the same project without her consistent support and her constant, searching challenges. I express my appreciation for her intellectual verve in the pages that follow. Ann Stoler likewise immediately took interest in this project, both through her inherent inquisitiveness and her distinctive manner of nurturing the projects and people that seem to convene and blossom around her. She read many drafts, always asking incisive questions, always insisting on clarity and clarification. Her reservations and her comprehension helped me to keep this project on even keel, and to bring it to fruition. This project became a book thanks, also, to the encouragement and promptings of Mary Murrell, who organized a panel on "The Stakes of Crisis" with me for the 2011 American Anthropology Association meeting, which helped me to see that this inquiry was not as eccentric as it seemed. Her sensitivity and sensibilities regarding "the book" are always sound guidance for me. And, as ever, Paul Rabinow precipitated the gestalt that allowed me to see past an early phase of this project: after reading a draft version of a long, exhaustive essay, he registered his enthusiasm for the project as well as its import, and then asked, with his characteristic sincerity, "But what's it about?"

I want to express immense gratitude to Bill Maurer for reading the draft manuscript from start to finish, for putting tough questions to me, and for giving me good advice, all of which made for a more thoughtful final version. I'm also very grateful to Orit Halpern, Jay Bernstein, Richard Bernstein, Gil Anidjar, Nicolas Langlitz, Ruth Marshall, Charles Piot, Tobias Rees, Julia Elyachar, and Robin Wagner-Pacifici for either reading drafts; giving me helpful comments, suggestions, and references; or discussing this project with me in different venues. Special, warm thanks likewise go to my colleagues in the anthropology department at the New School for Social Research— Ann Stoler, Lawrence Hirschfeld, Hugh Raffles, Miriam Ticktin, Nicolas Langlitz, Vyjayanthi Rao—all of whom have been awfully tolerant of this project, often censoring themselves each time they were about to say the word "crisis," but always keenly interested, and inevitably with humor. The graduate students at the New School have been equally interested and engaging, especially those who participated in the seminars I taught on topics related to this project, who took up the challenge of "crisis" in readings and term papers, and who were a great source of crisis comics. I'm indebted especially to Randi Irwin for tracking down articles and books, for proofreading, for preparing the index, for keeping me on track, and for her trustworthy advice.

Of course, over the past few years, many others have motivated and helped me in this project: Michel Callon, Jane Guyer, Adam Ashforth, Arjun Appadurai, the late Carol Breckenridge, Jean Comaroff, John Comaroff, Peter Geschiere, Doug Holmes, Stephen Collier, Paul Melton, Tim Marshall, Carol Wachs, Andrea Talmud, Béatrice Fraenkel, Nicolas Dodier, Frédéric Keck, Elisabeth Clavérie, Luc Boltan-ski, Catherine Alès, Jean-François Bayart, Béatrice Hibou, and Domi-nique Malaquais (who, in a phone conversation in 2007, said, "It's the anti-crisis!"). I owe very sincere thanks to Craig Calhoun, Sam Carter, and Jessica Coffey, who were exceptionally generous with me during my time as a Scholar-in-Residence at the Institute for Public Knowledge, New York University, where much of this manuscript was written. Thanks to Fred Dust and David Young for an overpriced one-minute consult. And to the Mud Truck on Astor Place . . .

I have benefited from exchanges with participants in many con-ferences and seminars, including: "Reworking Political Concepts. A Lexicon in Formation," the New School for Social Research and Columbia University Society of Fellows; "The Atlantic Studies Work-shop," Duke University; "The Stakes of Crisis," American Anthro-pology Association; Transitions Center, CNRS-NYU; "Un-disciplined Encounters: Science as a Terrain of Postcolonial Interaction be-tween Africa and Europe," the University of Ghent and Catholic Uni-versity of Leuven, University Foundation, Brussels; Department of Anthropology and Sociology, Swarthmore College; Anthropology Department, University of Chicago; "Rethinking Economic Anthro-pology: A Human Centred Approach," Economic and Social Research Council (UK), Department of Anthropology, London School of Eco-nomics; and the Franz Boas Lecture Series, Anthropology Depart-ment, Columbia University. Some of the material published herein appeared previously in "Crisis," *Political Concepts: A Critical Lexicon*: http://www.politicalconcepts.org/2011/crisis.

Ken Wissoker has been a delightful interlocutor and a careful edi-tor. I thank him for collaborating with me on this project with both anticipation and reassurance. I also want to express appreciation to the anonymous reviewers of the manuscript; their thorough readings and discerning questions were indispensable to me. And thanks also to Elizabeth Ault for her hard work on this publication.

I can't ever sufficiently express my gratitude to Gérard Roso for knowing that—no matter what—life cannot be crisis (*Ma petite entre-prise / Connaît pas la crise.*—Bashung). Thanks to him for affording time and space, for daring to know *l'impatience de la liberté*. And re-

sounding thanks go to Eva Roso and Rebecca Roso for their boister-
ous, clamorous, hurried, strident, impetuous . . . patience with me.
May they never know crisis.

This book is dedicated to Leonore and Harry Roitman, for their life
of books and the world, and their clarity.

WHAT IS AT STAKE?

Normalcy — Never Again
— MARTIN LUTHER KING JR.

"Normalcy, Never Again" is the title of the speech penned for an address to be delivered by Martin Luther King Jr. on the steps of the Lincoln Memorial on August 28, 1963. That day, however, Martin Luther King Jr. deviated from his "Normalcy — Never Again" text, instead improvising what is now known as the "I Have a Dream" speech.[1] I learned of the original, official title of his address on the very day of his birthday on January 15, 2009. Five days later, deeply conscious of King's legacy and his dream on the Washington Mall, Barack Obama, only just anointed as the forty-fourth president of the United States, defined contemporary American history in terms of crisis: "We are in the midst of crisis."[2]

Like King's "normalcy, never," Obama's crisis is used to characterize a moment in history so as to mark off a new age, or what is characterized as a "journey." This journey, defined by Obama in terms of "struggle" and "sacrifice," is historical insofar as it pertains to an economic and political conjuncture. And yet, after giving an inventory of the historical facts of crisis — homes lost, jobs shed, businesses shuttered — Obama added a qualifier: "These are the indicators of crisis," he said, "subject to data and statistics. Less measurable but no less profound is a sapping of confidence across our land—a nagging fear that America's decline is inevitable, and that the next generation must lower its sights." He then concluded: "This is the source of our confidence—the knowledge that God calls upon us to shape an uncertain destiny." Such knowledge in the face of uncertainty implies that the historical crisis entails, or perhaps constitutes, a transhistorical journey, being, as he insisted in his closing words, a matter of hope, promise, and grace: "With hope and virtue, let us brave once more the icy currents and endure what storms may come. Let it be said by our children's children that when we were tested we refused to let this journey end, that we did not turn our back nor did we falter; and with eyes fixed on the horizon and God's grace upon us, we carried forth that great gift of freedom and delivered it safely to future generations." Crisis is a historical event as much as it is an enduring condition of life and even the grounds for a transcendent human condition.

Obama noted in his address that the lived experience of what is deemed "crisis" should not be reduced to an ensemble of socioeconomic indicators. He sought to convey to the American public that he would face their present conditions of life as entailing an *experience* of crisis. His secular narrative of human history is conjugated with a Christian narrative of witnessing. And yet it clearly echoes self-described secular accounts in the social sciences that attempt to relate the ways in which history can be characterized *as* crisis; the ways that social life can be said to be *in* crisis; and the ways that crisis becomes an imperative, or a device for understanding how to act effectively in situations that belie, for the actors, a sense of possibility (Mbembe and Roitman 1995). But here the question arises: if crisis designates something more than a historical conjuncture, what is the status of that term? How did crisis, once a signifier for a critical, decisive moment, come to be construed as a protracted historical and experiential condition? The very idea of crisis as a condition suggests an ongoing state of affairs. But can one speak of a state of enduring crisis? Is this not an oxymoron?

In reflecting upon the status of this term as the most common and most pervasive qualifier of contemporary historical conditions—and manner of denoting "history" itself—this book sets the stage for a general inquiry into the status of "crisis" in social science theory and writing and therefore offers a departure, not a resolution.[3] In what follows, I am not concerned to theorize the term "crisis" or to come up with a working definition of it. Rather than essentialize it so as to make better use of it, I seek to understand the kinds of work the term "crisis" is or is not doing in the construction of narrative forms. Likewise, I am not concerned to demonstrate that crisis signifies something new in contemporary narrative accounts or that it now has a novel status in a history of ideas. I will not offer a review of the literature on crisis, nor will I show how contemporary usages of the term "crisis" are wrong and hence argue for a true, or more correct meaning.[4]

What I will consider is how crisis is constituted as an object of knowledge. Crisis is an omnipresent sign in almost all forms of narrative today; it is mobilized as the defining category of historical situations, past and present. The recent bibliography in the social sciences and popular press is vast; crisis texts are a veritable industry.[5] The geography of crisis has come to be world geography CNN-style: crisis in Afghanistan, crisis in Darfur, crisis in Iran, crisis in Iraq, crisis in the Congo, crisis in Cairo, crisis in the Middle East, crisis on Main Street. But beyond global geopolitics, crisis qualifies the very nature of events: humanitarian crisis, environmental crisis, energy crisis, debt crisis, financial crisis, and so forth. Through the term "crisis," the singularity of events is abstracted by a generic logic, making crisis a term that seems self-explanatory. As I hope to make clear in what follows, crisis serves as the noun-formation of contemporary historical narrative; it is a non-locus from which to claim access to both history and knowledge of history. In other words, crisis is mobilized in narrative constructions to mark out or to designate "moments of truth"; it is taken to be a means to access historical truth, and even a means to think "history" itself. Such moments of truth are often defined as turning points in history, when decisions are taken or events are decided, thus establishing a particular teleology. And similarly, though seemingly without recourse to teleology, crisis moments are defined as instances when normativity is laid bare, such as when the contingent or partial quality of knowledge claims—principles, suppositions, premises, criteria, and logical or causal relations—are disputed, critiqued, challenged, or disclosed. It follows that crisis is posited as an epistemological impasse and, as we will see below, is claimed to found the possibility for other historical trajectories or even for a (new) future.

Barack Obama invoked the revelatory power of crisis in this way: as a moment that reveals truth, the crisis denoted by the limits—or "bursting"—of the so-called financial bubble divulged alleged "false value" and offered the hope of reestablishing or relocating "true value," or what we like to think of as the fundamentals of the economy and the proper trajectory of history, both being dependent on adequate knowledge claims. As a category denoting a moment of truth in this way, and despite presumptions that crisis does not imply, in itself, a definite direction of change, the term "crisis" signifies a diagnostic of the present; it implies a certain telos because it is inevitably, though most often implicitly, directed toward a norm. Evoking crisis entails reference to a norm because it requires a comparative state for judgment: crisis compared to what? That question evokes the significance of crisis as an axiological problem, or the questioning of the epistemological or ethical grounds of certain domains of life and thought.

This book inquires into the significance of crisis in-and-of-itself. Instead of starting with particular crises—the crisis of Africa, the financial crisis, the crisis of subjectivity, the neoliberal crisis—and then rushing to explain their causes and fundaments, I first ask questions of the concept of crisis itself.[6] To do so, I explore how we think crisis came to be a historical concept: I ask how crisis achieves its status as a historico-philosophical concept and I ask how we practice that very premise in narrations of history and in the determinations of what even counts as history. To explore the orthodoxy of crisis—the conventional historiography of the term and its consequential practice—I take an impudent and somewhat puzzling step. In the pages that follow, we meet up with Reinhart Koselleck and Robert Shiller, Thomas Hobbes and David Harvey, John Locke and Michael Lewis, the Masonic lodges and the hedge fund managers. We shift from prophecy and prognosis to risk-based pricing and adjustable rate mortgages, from epochal consciousness to asset bubbles, from judgment and critique to foreclosures and forbearance. We move between the conceptual history of crisis and the practice of crisis analysis, from historiography to contemporary financial history. There is no rush to explain the crisis. Instead, what follows is a deliberate review of the conventional account of the emergence of crisis as a historico-philosophical concept and examination of how that concept is therefore practiced in contemporary accounts of financial crisis, permitting and enabling certain narrations and giving rise to certain questions, but not others.

While most financial analysts and homeowners are not necessarily aware of the historico-philosophical status of the term "crisis," this book indicates that the lines drawn between academic and popular crisis narrations are not as bold as is presumed. This book attempts to erase, or at least lighten, those lines. It does so by putting on par academic analyses of financial crisis and so-called popular accounts of financial crisis. In 2007–9, accession to crisis—or credence in the claim that "this is crisis"—led to a frenzy of academic analyses, which included economists, sociologists, political scientists, historians, and anthropologists, all attempting to explain "the crisis." It likewise inspired a host of journalistic and novelistic accounts of the financial crisis of 2007–9.[7] A cross-reading of these literatures gives insight into how the technical "facts" of the financial crisis become folk wisdom or, better, tacit knowledge—and this, despite the "mutually inconsistent narratives" that can be gleaned from the dizzying variety of accounts (Lo 2012). Indeed, the very distinction between expert and lay relies on stable subject positions that are not tenable. Where, for instance, do we draw the lines between experts and laypersons, academics and commoners? Accountants and corporate managers are not necessarily academic economists, but are they considered laypersons with respect to financial analysis? Are lawyers, engineers, and mathematicians working in private nonfinancial firms or laboratories to be considered laypersons in contrast to academic economists and financial analysts? Are economic anthropologists housed in universities laypersons in relation to their colleagues in economics departments?

One might reply that the real laypersons are those holding mortgages, those who have been foreclosed upon. But even here, the dark line drawn between academic and lay must be blanched. In his brilliant, carefully crafted elaboration of an anthropology of the contemporary, Paul Rabinow explains and illustrates the "mode of adjacency" necessary to anthropological inquiry, the goal of which is "identifying, understanding, and formulating something actual *neither by directly identifying with it nor by making it exotic*" (2008, 49, my emphasis). He notes the disjuncture between "those authorized to pronounce prescriptive speech acts" and those who are not—between, let's say, financial analysts and journalists, on the one hand, and homeowners, on the other. And he concludes (79): "Thus, while many of the serious speech acts about the moral landscape are produced by actors who are reflective about their own positions, the anthropologist can approach their discourses and practices like those of any other. Theorists, philosophers, ethicists, scientists, and the like can thus qualify for inclusion in the category that used to be called 'natives.'"[8] While the present book is not based on anthropological fieldwork of the practitioners of crisis analysis, it takes its cue from Rabinow's sense of "untimely work." I suspend judgment about expert claims to crisis so as to see how those very (expert) claims and (lay) accession to those claims serve not radical change, as expected with crisis, but rather the affirmation of long-standing principles, thereby precluding certain thoughts and acts, such as the *outright refutation of the very idea of foreclosure* as a germane or valid concept and action. This book tacks between the historiography of the concept of crisis and recent interpretations of what is now known as the subprime mortgage crisis, excavating the epistemological bases for certain claims ("this is crisis") and reflecting upon how those claims engender certain types of action or practice (devaluation, foreclosure) and not others (human protest-chains around homes, the denial of the very legibility of the terms "foreclosure" and "forbearance"). In that way, this book is out of synch with the "hyperoccupied lives" (Rabinow 2008, 47) of those producing feverish crisis pronouncements, urgent crisis analyses, and clamorous crisis pamphlets—out of step with those seeking to manage or overcome the crisis.

Both Martin Luther King Jr. and Barack Obama attempt to inaugurate new historical times with reference to the concept of crisis. The redemptive and utopian quality of their historical narrations speaks to the normative and teleological nature of the concept of crisis, which, taken to be the grounds for both the human sciences and critique, is likewise construed as the grounds for transformative action, as will be made clear below.

The following account of the ways in which crisis is conceived as a historical concept—as both a particular entry point into history and as a means to reveal historical truth—makes clear how crisis is posited "as" history itself. In other words, in the social sciences, when history is taken to be immanent to social relations, crisis serves as the term that enables the very elaboration of such history. This founding role of the concept of crisis in social science narration and in the constitution and elaboration of history itself is set forth by the late German historian Reinhart Koselleck, author of perhaps the only conceptual history of crisis, which thus serves as the authoritative historiography. As I outline in detail in the chapters that follow, Koselleck provides an illustration of the temporalization of history, or the emergence of "history" as a temporal category. He attributes the emergence of the category of history as a temporality to the concomitant displacement of the term "crisis," arguing that, by the end of the eighteenth century, crisis is the basis for the claim that one can judge history by means of a diagnosis of time. Koselleck likewise maintains that both this claim and this judgment entail a specific historical consciousness— *a consciousness that posits history as a temporality upon which one can act.* For this historical consciousness, crisis is a criterion for what counts as "history"; crisis signifies change, such that crisis "is" history; and crisis designates "history" as such. In this way, crisis achieves the status of a historico-philosophical concept; it is the means by which history is located, recognized, comprehended, and even posited.

I take Reinhart Koselleck's remarkable conceptual history of crisis to be indicative of the practice of the concept of crisis. His account of how crisis achieves status as a historico-philosophical concept likewise illustrates the practice of the premise of crisis, or how it serves a set of interlocking determinations: what counts as an event, the status of an event, the qualification of history itself, and the basis of narration. I refer to Koselleck's conceptual history on two registers: as the orthodox historiography of the term and as an account that, itself, partakes of a conventional practice of historiography, which presupposes criteria for what counts as an event and premises as to what can be narrated—or the means to distinguish between "a properly historical account of reality and a nonhistorical or ahistorical or antihistorical account" (White 2002, xii). Less concerned with the question of whether or not Koselleck's rendering of the emergence of historical consciousness is correct or accurate, I dwell instead on the question of *how the term "crisis" is posited* as fundamental to this very idea of historical consciousness and to a metaphysics of history. My point is not that crisis is false or merely a constructed basis for narration; my aim is to raise questions about the status of the concept of crisis as a founding term for the elaboration of "history" per se—history being the ultimate locus of significance and the ontological status of historical temporality being taken for granted. In its practice, as we learn from Koselleck, crisis is figured as judgment: judging time in terms of analogous intervals and judging history in terms of its significance. But it equally serves expectations for world-immanent justice, or the faith that history is the ultimate form of judgment. I ask herein—inspired by Koselleck and yet putting the question to him, as well: what is the burden of proof for such judgments?

By way of response, I consider the forms of critique that are necessarily engendered by crisis narrations. Critique and crisis are cognates, as Reinhart Koselleck (1988) reminds us: crisis is the basis of social and critical theory. Being bound to its cognate (critique), the concept of crisis denotes the prevailing and fairly peculiar belief that history could be alienated in terms of its philosophy—that one could perceive a dissonance between historical events and representations of those events. Crisis-claims evoke a moral demand for a difference between the past and the future. And crisis-claims evoke the possibility for new forms of historical subjectivity, transpiring through determinations of the limits of reason and knowledge. That is, crisis, or the disclosure of epistemological limits, occasions critique. This desire for (temporal) difference is described by scholars new and old as a moral task or an ethical demand, being based on a perceived discrepancy between nature and reason, technical developments and moral positioning, knowledge and human interests, constituted categories and epistemological limits, or a critical consciousness of the present state of affairs.[9] No matter its quality, the discrepancy is taken to be an aporia; it establishes the formal or logical possibility of crisis. And in all cases, both prognosis and the very apprehension of history are defined by the negative occupation of an immanent world: *what went wrong?* For critical historical consciousness—or the specific, historical way of knowing the world has "history"—historical significance is discerned in terms of epistemological or ethical failure. Without an inviolate transcendental realm—God, reason, truth—from which to signify human history, or because observation takes place from within immanence, we effectively assume a negative occupation of the immanent world.[10]

By excavating the crisis term in the critique-and-crisis cognate, by marking their co-constitution, I hope to draw attention to the means by which crisis serves as a distinction or transcendental placeholder in the occupation of an immanent world. In the words of William Rasch (2002, 20), inspired by Niklas Luhmann, "In a world where descriptions proliferate and faith in the authority of reason has gone the way of faith in the authority of God, contingency becomes the transcendental placeholder."[11] As we will see below, crisis serves as a transcendental placeholder because it is a means for signifying contingency; it is a term that allegedly allows one to think the "otherwise." Though not concerned with the term "crisis," Rasch presents my point of departure clearly: "If . . . moral codes (commandments), Holy Scripture, papal and royal edicts, and the voice of prophets and visionaries no longer deliver direct evidence of the transcendent realm, but rather become historicized and seen as socially constructed artifacts, the task of reclaiming authority must be negotiated within the domain of an immanence that has been loosed from its transcendent anchorage. The world is as it is, but it could be otherwise. *How that 'otherwise' is to be thought* becomes the 'quasi-transcendental' task of an immanence trying to think itself" (Rasch 2000, 130, my emphasis). The concept of crisis is crucial to the "how" of thinking otherwise. And as a term that serves the practice of unveiling supposed underlying contradictions, or latencies, it is a distinction that transcends oppositions and dichotomies. Therefore, this book designates anti-crisis: there is not "crisis" versus "noncrisis," both of which can be observed empirically; rather, crisis is a logical observation that generates meaning in a self-referential system, or a non-locus from which to signify contingency and paradox.[12] And the judgment of crisis is necessarily a post hoc interrogation: what went wrong? Crisis is posited as an a priori; the grounds for knowledge of crisis are neither questioned nor made explicit. And hence contemporary narratives of crisis elude two questions: How can one *know* crisis in history? And how can one *know* crisis itself?

Crisis is a historical "super concept" (*Oberbegriffe*) (Koselleck 2006, 392) that, to my mind, raises questions rather than facilitating answers. If crisis denotes a critical, decisive moment, or a turning point, does this not imply a certain philosophy of history? And what does it take to posit the very idea that meaning or thought can be in a state of crisis? Moreover, when crisis is posited as the very condition of contemporary situations, is it not the case that certain questions become possible while others are foreclosed? This book explores these questions.

To do so, we embark on a trek over the anxious terrain of crisis narration. This trek is one of observation: we observe how academic and nonacademic observers themselves observe economic and financial actors, both human and technical, which they locate, define, and interpret as having produced crisis. We observe, then, the blind spot of second-order observation. Moreover, through this survey of the practice of crisis in contemporary narrations of "the 2007–9 financial crisis," we see how accession to crisis engenders certain narrations and note how the term enables and forecloses various kinds of questions. Through this review of a host of recent narratives of financial crisis, I am not seeking to establish the relative veracity of these accounts; I am not interested in whether or not certain purported explanations of "the crisis" are more or less tenable. Although I do explore questions relating to the production of value and risk, and the status of subprime and houses, I do so only insofar as these terms constitute the grammar of financial crisis narratives. The point of this grand tour of crisis narratives is not to determine the best way to decipher the crisis or to establish who "got it right" in recent analyses. The point is to demonstrate how the term "crisis" establishes the conditions of possible histories and to indicate how it is a blind spot in social science narrative constructions.

We thus take a journey through a wide-ranging array of interpretations, each of which claims a particular tradition: liberal economy, neo-Keynesian, neo-Marxist, cultural studies, and cultural economy. All proceed from the question, what went wrong? All search for origins, sources, roots, causes, reasons . . . none waver in their faith in crisis, a term that is posited without question or doubt. All seek to demonstrate deviations from the proper course of history and distortions in human knowledge and practice—the discrepancy between the world and human knowledge of the world. Crisis signifies a purportedly observable chasm between "the real," on the one hand, and what is variously portrayed in the accounts reviewed below as fictitious, erroneous, or an illogical departure from the real, on the other. The chasm signifies a supposed dissonance between empirical history and a philosophy of history—between truly grounded material value, on the one hand, and hypothetical judgments and evaluations, on the other.[13] What is at issue is our alienation from history and the potential for revelation of true value and the true significance of events—of redemption, emancipation, deliverance. I ask: how can we claim to represent that chasm? What is the basis of a claim to know the locus of our alienation from underlying value, from material value, from real value, from truth value?

To conclude this expedition over the terrain of crisis narration, I put a set of particularly pragmatic questions to the narratives that I review herein: When does a credit (asset) become a debt (toxic asset)? How do we distinguish the former from the latter? *At what point* do houses figured as equity become figured as a debt? *At what point* do subprime mortgage bonds transform from an asset to a liability? And the ultimate question: When does the judgment of crisis obtain? We see, by putting these questions to contemporary crisis narratives, how crisis, in itself, cannot be located or observed as an object of first-order knowledge. The observation "money" is a first-order observation based on a distinction (money/not money); the statements "I lost money" or "Lost money is a crisis" are second-order observations. A first-order observation (money) does not indicate how the distinction (money/not money) was made; and the distinction (how the observation was made) is necessarily the object of a second-order observation.[14] But taking note of crisis as a distinction, or as a second-order operation, does not amount to denying crisis. *The point is to take note of the effects of the claim to crisis, to be attentive to the effects of our very accession to that judgment.* Crisis engenders certain forms of critique, which politicize interest groups. This is a politics of crisis. Would not crisis, if it effectively obtained, engender not merely critique of existing relations and practices, but rather occasion the reorganization and transformation of the very boundary between "the economic" and "the political," and, more significant, the transformation of the *very intelligibility* of constitutive terms, such as "debt," "liquidity," and "risk"? In assuming crisis as a point of departure, we remain closed off in a politics of crisis. We can ask, echoing the Occupy Wall Street movement, who should bear the burden of fading prosperity? But other constitutive questions, related to the production of effective practice, remain unarticulated, such as, how did debt come to be figured as an asset class in the first place?

To answer this latter question, I turn to the few studies of the production of value through market devices and financial infrastructures that help us to account for the *efficacy of economic and financial practices*, which sustain the production of value—*figured as debt*. Here, instead of financial crisis due to irrational speculation, corrupt culture, erroneous policy, faulty regulation, defective models, missed forecasting, or systemic failure and underlying contradictions, we have an accounting of specific practices and the production of positive—or, better, practical—knowledge, such that the claim to crisis becomes a particular (political) solution to what is declared a problem for certain domains of life. These rare observations of the production of economic and financial value without positing crisis help us to grasp how "crisis" is less a claim about error in valuation than a judgment about value. But noncrisis accounts cannot be taken as distinct "alternative" narrations insofar as they do not provide evidence against "X account of crisis" so as to prove or affirm "Y account of crisis." In that sense, my turn to these accounts is a thought experiment: this exercise explores the grounds of narrative without crisis, but these are not alternative explanations because crisis is not their object. Doubtless, this thought experiment risks reproducing the "problem of meaning"—or the belief that there is a discrepancy between history and representations of history—insofar as it raises the possibility of narrating history otherwise.[15] But here I want to underscore that critique and crisis are cognates, and so want to bring to our attention the forms of critique engendered by crisis narratives. We see that these forms of critique rest on assumptions about how categories like "the market" or "finance" *should* function and therefore generate conjecture about how deviations from "true" market or financial value were produced; they do not account for the ways that such value is produced in the first place. In other words, when crisis is posited as an a priori, it obviates accounts of *positive, pragmatic* spaces of calculative possibility. I therefore raise the possibility of noncrisis narratives and explore how possible, alternative narratives about houses and their worth might be generated without recourse to a "sociology of error" (Bloor 1991, 12), without constructing a post hoc narrative of denunciation or post hoc judgments of deviation and failure.[16]

Ultimately, I invite the reader to put less faith in crisis, which means asking what is at stake with crisis in-and-of-itself. "Crisis" is a term that is bound up in the predicament of signifying human history, often serving as a transcendental placeholder in ostensible solutions to that problem. In that sense, the term "crisis" serves as a primary enabling blind spot for the production of knowledge. That is, crisis is a point of view, or an observation, which itself is not viewed or observed. I apprehend the concept of crisis through the metaphor of a blind spot so as to apprehend crisis as an observation that, like all observations or cognitions, does not account for the very conditions of its observation.[17] Consequentially, making that blind spot visible means asking questions about how we produce significance for ourselves. At least, it means asking about how we produce "history." At most, it means asking how we might construct accounts without discerning historical significance in terms of ethical failure. Thus we might ask: what kind of narrative could be produced where meaning is not everywhere a problem?[18] An answer to that question, no matter how improbable, as we will see below, requires, as a first, inaugural step, consideration of the ways in which crisis, as an enabling blind spot for the production of knowledge, entails unremitting and often implicit judgment about latencies, or errors and failings that must be eradicated and, evidently hopefully, overcome.

CHAPTER 1

CRISIS DEMANDS

JUDGMENT DAY

"What does it mean, and what does it take to envisage a society as *breaking down?*" This is Michael Taussig's question (1992, 17, emphasis in original), which he puts to himself in his reflections on terror in Colombia during the 1990s. In thinking alongside him, I de-emphasize the problem of meaning and the process of breakdown, such that the question becomes, *what does it take* to envisage society as breaking down? Such visions could only arise in counter-distinction to imagined alternative societies. Without them, we could not allow for such a judgment: the affirmation "this society is breaking down" requires a comparison, a comparative state of affairs.

The very etymology of the term "crisis" speaks to that requirement of judgment. Though the details of its semantic history can be found in many places, it is worth reiterating that its etymology is said to originate with the ancient Greek term *krinô* (to separate, to choose, cut, to decide, to judge), which suggested a definitive decision. It is said to have had significance in the domains of law, medicine, and theology, with the medical signification prevailing by the fifth and fourth centuries BC. Associated with the Hippocratic school (*Corpus Hippocratum*) as part of a medical grammar, crisis denoted the turning point of a disease, or a critical phase in which life or death was at stake and called for an irrevocable decision. Significantly, crisis was not the disease or illness per se; it was the condition that *called for* decisive judgment between alternatives. But the term "crisis" no longer clearly signifies a singular moment of decisive judgment; we now presume that crisis is a condition, a state of affairs, an experiential category. Today, crisis is posited as a protracted and potentially persistent state of ailment and demise.

And yet, while crisis serves as the basis of a great deal of writing on topics ranging from conjunctural affairs to the human condition, extremely scant attention has been given to the conceptual histories of the term.[1] Indeed, we have but one significant conceptual history, elaborated by Reinhart Koselleck and now taken to be the conventional historiography of the term. His inquiry into how crisis achieves status as a historico-philosophical concept gives insight into how we practice the premise of crisis—how it serves an ensemble of interlocking determinations: what counts as an event, the status of an event, the qualification of history itself, and the basis of narration. Koselleck is best known as a founder and practitioner of *Begriffsgeschichte*, a practice of historiography devoted to the study of the fundamental concepts that have given rise to, and partake of, a specific concept of "history" and a distinctly historical consciousness.[2] Koselleck is crucially concerned with the historicity of concepts and the emergence of historical self-understanding, or what he takes to be the development of historical consciousness—the philosophical and experiential awareness of one's own historical formation and of the historical quality of that knowledge itself. Through this "cultural achievement," the concept of history emerges as a philosophical and experiential category: "European society began to think and act as if it existed in history, as if its 'historicity' was a feature, if not the defining feature of its identity" (White 2002, x). Koselleck characterizes this emergence in terms of discontinuity and rupture; historical consciousness marks off *Neuzeit* (the modern age, modernity) and prompts a guiding question for conceptual history: what kind of *experience* is entailed by this historical consciousness? (Koselleck 2004; and cf. Tribe 2004, xvii). He asserts (2002, 111), for instance, that the production of historical time "is subjectively enacted in humans as historical beings," by which he means that there is a consequent "compulsion to coordinate past and future so as to be able to live at all."³ The experience of this temporal differentiation between past and future generates a concomitant differential between experience and expectation—the source of crisis. For Koselleck, *Neuzeit* is experienced as problematic—riddled with crisis or in permanent crisis—because of the constant, allegedly accelerating production of both this open future and the utopian hope of fulfillment.⁴

Koselleck is interested in the semantic power of concepts; concepts impart meaning and experience in relation to a complex semantic network, through which we can apprehend historical transformations. In tracing this emergence of historical consciousness and *Neuzeit* as an experience of crisis, his conceptual history of crisis describes a decisive shift in the semantics of the term, which he claims transpired between Hippocratic medical grammar and Christian exegesis.⁵ Not surprisingly, one did not replace the other: in the elaboration of Christian theology, with reference to the New Testament and alongside Aristotelian legal language, *krisis* was paired with *judicium* and came to signify judgment before God, which Koselleck characterizes as possibly the unsurpassable signification of crisis in the course of its conceptual history (2002, 237; 2006, 358–59).⁶ Through the history of its conceptual displacements—involving the elaboration of semantic webs as opposed to a linear development of substitutions, and which I have drastically abbreviated⁷—the term "crisis" entailed a prognosis, which increasingly came to imply a prognosis of time.

Koselleck's conceptual history of crisis illustrates how, over the course of the eighteenth century, a spatial metaphor comes to be a historical concept through the temporalization of the Last Judgment. His account of this complex semantic shift is part of his larger oeuvre on the emergence of the European concept of history and the ways in which associated historico-political concepts (e.g., progress) thematize time.⁸ Koselleck argues that prior to the achievement of this shift, crisis did not have a time; it was not historically dated and it did not signify historical dates. While throughout the seventeenth century the term had a range of political applications related to the body politic, constitutional order, and military situations, by the late eighteenth century, its religious connotation is exacerbated, though in a "post-theological mode," or as a philosophy of history (Kosel-leck 2006, 370). Through its semantic history, crisis, as a concept, sheds its apocalyptic meaning: "It turns into a structural category of Christianly understood history pure and simple; eschatology is, so to speak, historically monopolized" (2002, 242).[9]

With the temporalization of history—or the process by which, since the late eighteenth century, time is no longer figured as a medium in which histories take place, but rather is itself conceived as having a historical quality—history no longer occurs in time; rather, time itself becomes an active, transformative (historical) principle ([1979] 2004, 236, and 2002, 165–67). For Koselleck, the temporalization of the Last Judgment is the temporalization of history: prophecy is displaced by prognosis.[10] According to this (highly contested) inter-pretation (which relies on a "Christian conception of supersession"), prophecy involves symbols of what is already known and entails ex-pectation in constant similitude while prognosis, to the contrary, gen-erates novel events.[11] Rational prognosis related to intrinsic possibili-ties hinges on an imagined novel time that is in flight.[12] Crisis serves this transposition from prophecy to prognosis, or the "channeling of millennial expectations," because it becomes the basis for claims that one can interpret the entire course of history via a diagnosis of time.

Such evaluations about a putative temporal situation require knowl-edge of both the past and the future, which implies that, as a concept that has been integral to the temporalization of history, crisis entails a theory of time. In effect, time is constituted as historical through crisis; more than just a novel manner of defining and representing history per se, the temporalization of history amounts to a tempo-ral shift in experience.[13] The very notion of a historical perspective, which allows for the identification and judgment of a temporal situa-tion, presupposes that history has a temporal quality. And, in similar fashion, the historical perspective itself is taken to have a temporal quality, making the truth of history contingent, not given once and for all. That now familiar point is based on the assumption that time is constantly being produced and that it is always new: the future is fundamentally open.[14]

But this constant production of the new, or of new time, is not without the production of new pasts. In order to incorporate new experiences into one's own history—inspired by the awareness of an elsewhere and by the very idea that one constructs history, or in order to account for nonsimultaneous (diverse) and yet simultaneous (chronologically) histories[15]—one must be able to conceive of the past in terms of its radical or fundamental difference. Crisis comes to signify the marking out of "new time" insofar as it denotes a unique, immanent transition phase, or a specific historical epoch. The somewhat odd practice of the retrospective recognition of the past as new—an epoch can only be recognized as such (i.e., in its "true significance" for history) ex post facto—allegedly distinguishes this "epochal consciousness" and the philosophy of history of the late eighteenth century. In effect, Koselleck's account of this historical consciousness and philosophy of history presupposes that, because time is not manifest and thus cannot be intuited, we necessarily draw on terms from the spatial realm. This notion of time as a formal, a priori condition of intuition, associated with Kant, can be contrasted to a notion of subjective historical times, or simultaneous, plural objects defined by their own measure. Koselleck's point is that historical concepts are dependent upon metaphorical language and a spatial referent: "To talk about history and time is difficult for a reason that has to do with more than 'history.' Time cannot be intuited (*ist anschauungslos*). If a historian brings past events back to mind through his language, then the listener or reader will perhaps associate an intuition with them as well. But does he thereby have an intuition of past *time*? Hardly so, or only in a metaphorical use of language, for instance, in the sense in which one speaks of the time of the French Revolution without thereby making visible anything specifically temporal" (Koselleck 2002, 102). And of course the temporal significance of such concepts is always experienced and apprehended in terms of retrospective effects.[16]

Crisis, as a historical concept, refers to the retrospective effects of events and to their constitutive presuppositions. For what Koselleck calls the "epochal consciousness" that arises by the late eighteenth century, crisis is a criterion for *what counts* as "history" and it is a means of signifying change. It is a means of designating history in-

and-of-itself.[17] While typical to an eighteenth-century philosophy of history and a corresponding conceptualization of history in terms of progress, this epochal consciousness is nevertheless very familiar to us; it is in keeping with contemporary usage of the term as a turning point in any particular history, or as an iterative, periodizing concept. In this instance, crisis is defined as both entirely specific (because it defines a historical epoch) and as structural recurrence (because it establishes and fulfills the notion that historical change takes place in analogous forms). In sum, crisis acquires a historico-philosophical dimension and becomes, by the end of the eighteenth century, a free-standing historico-philosophical concept. Thereafter, one speaks of crisis pure and simple; it is the means by which history can be located and understood.[18] This history, which is for Koselleck specifically "modern," is constituted out of its own conditions of knowledge and action: the criteria of time.[19] This new concept of history in-and-for-itself nonetheless requires a referent from which movement, transformation, and change—historical change itself—can be posited. It is in that sense that crisis is the means to "access" history and to qualify "history" as such: crisis marks history and crisis generates history.

What we forget when invoking this technical or scholastic sense of the term is its theological genealogy, which Koselleck recalls: this manner of marking both a threshold and the possibility of analogous forms that translate specificity into a general logic is the occasion for the claim to "offer historically immanent patterns of interpretation for crises that are theoretically able to do without the intervention of God" (2002, 24; and see 2004, 40–41, 240; 2006, 371).[20] Koselleck affirms a secularization narrative and a Christian conception of supersession that is nicely recapitulated by Kathleen Davis (2008, 18): "Wrested from God and claimed for the 'world,' time only becomes truly historical through a political-theological tear that inaugurates a new 'age'—a tear that thereby defines the relation of the world and time, and that paradoxically occupies a transcendent position by virtue of banishing transcendence." Crisis serves that narrative, as Koselleck maintains, but it *thereby* becomes, as Davis says with respect to the practice of historical periodization, "its own logic, a self-identity that, through rupture rather than through presence, supplies the necessary platform for a claim to sovereignty" (2008, 18).[21] To be sure, acquiescence to the truth of the notion of history as immanent does not imply that history is no longer postulated as a predicament. With reference to a host of witnesses of the impending or affirmed crises, including Robespierre, Rousseau, Diderot, Thomas Paine, Burke, Herder, Fichte, Saint-Simon, Auguste Comte, Lorenz von Stein, Schleiermacher, Schlegel, and Marx and Engels, Koselleck declares: "That the crisis in which one currently finds oneself could be the last, great, and unique decision, after which history would look entirely different in the future—this semantic option is taken up *more and more frequently* the less the absolute end of history is believed to be approaching with the Last Judgment. To this extent, it is a question of recasting a theological principle of belief. It is expected of world-immanent history itself" (2002, 243, my emphasis; and see 2002, 243–44; 2006, 370–97).

What is expected of history? With the temporalization of the Last Judgment, history, in its immanence, becomes a problem of meaning. If the emergence of crisis as a historical concept occluded practices of prophecy in favor of practices of prognosis, as Koselleck argues, this raises the issue of the burden of proof for meaning in history, and for the meaning, or significance, of history itself. Koselleck comments on this burden of proof, invoking Schiller's influential dictum: "World history is the judgment of the world."[22]

> This model is compatible with fate, which in Herodotus appears behind all individual histories and which can be read again and again as the consummation of a world-immanent justice. However, Schiller's dictum raises a greater claim. An inherent justice, one which acquires almost a magical air, is not only required of individual histories but of all world history in toto. Logically, every injustice, every incommensurability, every unatoned crime, every senselessness and uselessness is apodictically excluded. Thus the burden of proof for the meaning of this history increases enormously. It is no longer historians who, because of their better knowledge, believe themselves to be able to morally judge the past

ex post facto, but rather it is assumed that history, as an acting subject, enforces justice. (2002, 241; 2006, 371)[23]

Through the invocation of the term "crisis" as a historically unique transition phase, which would mark an epoch, historical experience is likewise generalized as a logical recurrence—the historian is the judge of events. And yet history itself is posited as serving the *ultimate* form of judgment, a judgment we take to be effected, retrospectively, through acts and errors. (Tellingly and perhaps evocatively, Schiller's dictum originated in a love poem he composed about a missed opportunity.) But knowledge about that past—glorious consummation or disgraced failure—distinguishes the possible, open future, which is a problem. Judging time (sorting change from stasis, perceiving intervals) and judging history (diagnosing demise or improvement, defining winners and losers) is a matter of prognosis. And such prognosis depends upon the stabilization of "a single concept limited to the present with which to capture a new era that may have various temporal beginnings and whose unknown future seems to give free scope to all sorts of wishes and anxieties, fears and hope" (Koselleck 2006, 372).

THE MORAL DEMAND

The very notion that one could judge historical time (that it presents itself to us as an objective entity to be judged) and that history is defined by a teleology of justice (that there are winners and losers, errors and victories) conjures an extraordinarily self-conscious mode of being. The emergence of this particular form of historical self-consciousness is the motivating spirit of Reinhart Koselleck's overall intellectual project; but it is most notably the subject of his remarkable first book, *Critique and Crisis*, in which he presents a conceptual history of the mutual constitution of those cognates: critique and crisis.[24] His aim is to illustrate that this historical self-consciousness is related to what he defines as a specifically "modern" attitude toward politics.[25] Koselleck is fundamentally interested in what constitutes politics, as is reflected in his accounting of the emergence of historical consciousness in terms of contestation over concepts.

Koselleck apprehends this contestation through two key terms: morality and politics. He puts forth the counterintuitive argument that over the course of the eighteenth century, a novel distinction was formulated between the respective categories of morality and politics, which allowed for what he terms the "exclusion of morality from politics" and what he takes to be the Enlightenment style of critique. His lengthy rendering of the positions and debates that ran the course of at least a century both assembles and differentiates various celebrated figures: Barclay, d'Aubigné, Hobbes, Locke, Simon, Bayle, Schiller, Voltaire, Diderot, the Illuminati, the *Encyclopédistes*, Turgot, Rousseau, Raynal, Paine. He intends to relate the now familiar story of the emergence of a bourgeois public (an account most frequently attributed to Jürgen Habermas), or to account for the emergent "self-understanding" of this public as a distinct realm that constitutes "society" and is invested with Natural Law, thus marking off a self-proclaimed "moral society" from politics.[26] The disassociation between political and moral authority that he describes is generally assumed to be an actual foundational moment in Western intellectual history, marking off what has been called "The Great Separation," or "The Crisis" that allegedly marks off new time—that of secular history (cf. for example, Lilla 2007).[27] This much critiqued "triumphalist history of the secular" (Asad 1993, 25) assumes the effective disassociation between the religious and the political realms, between the juridical and the religious, or between political and moral authority.[28]

Thus this apparent contradiction in terms, this "anti-political politics" put forth by Koselleck as the *basis for critique*, is contingent upon acceptance of *the notion that morality marks out a pre-political or non-political realm*: "The internal and fundamental precondition for anti-state activity, namely the moral distancing from politics, becomes transformed into the ostensibly non-political basis of the fight against Absolutism" (Koselleck 1988, 96). This notional separation between morality (conscience) and politics (the state) has *consequences for manners of positing social change*, which come to be understood as transpiring through changes in moral positions, or via rational persuasion and the telos of reason, and thus from *outside* the institutions of the state. Thus, by way of illustration, Koselleck describes the conversion of the Masonic lodges and the Republic of Letters from "enclaves of internal exile" in the realm of the absolutist state to "centres of moral authority" in eighteenth-century France. In the political transformation of these moral societies, claims to "political legitimacy [grow] out of moral innocence" (Koselleck 1988, 95)[29]—a statement about politics that rings as a truism to our twenty-first-century ears, perhaps most recently in Barack Obama's inauguration speech.

Of course, as I have signaled already, one can put many questions to Koselleck's historiography. Does he not assume both the efficacy and historical adequacy of "the Enlightenment" as a political project? Does he not assume a premodern versus modern distinction, which could be undermined via alternative periodizations, categorizations, and narratives? Does he not make use of particular personae as reductive examples of a style of thought? Does he not portray the distinction between morality and politics in absolute terms, which is a fallacy? Doesn't his conceptual history partake of a teleological understanding of historical development? And does he not affirm a misleading—and even Orientalist—divide between modern historical consciousness, on the one hand, and a theological Middle Ages incapable of history, on the other?[30]

Bedrich Loewenstein (1976), for example, takes issue with Koselleck's depiction of an "absolute contrast" between morality and politics, and raises the question of the historical adequacy of the Enlightenment project. I agree entirely with his point that Koselleck does not question the historical adequacy of the Enlightenment as a political project. However, the norms of reason and humanity still serve as principles of justification for politics, or for a form of political utopia, today, as Loewenstein himself acknowledges.[31] More significantly, although in related manner, Koselleck's brand of transition narrative is grounded in a fundamental period division between a theologically determined Middle Ages, which supposedly does not apprehend historical temporality, on the one hand, and a modern historical consciousness, which is allegedly determined by the apprehension of historical temporality, on the other (Davis 2008). The presumption or substantiation of this divide between the religious Middle Ages (the religious past) and secular modernity (the secular present) maps onto the geopolitical divide between a timeless elsewhere and a fully historical present (Said 1979; Fabian 1983; Asad 1998, 2003; Anidjar 2006; and especially Davis 2008).[32]

These reasons to take issue with Koselleck's narration of the emergence of historical consciousness gesture to questions we can also ask about the status of the concept of crisis in historical narration—most obviously, its role as an iterative, periodizing concept. But we can likewise note that Koselleck's preoccupation is not fundamentally empirical; he seeks to thematize emergence, or the prospect of radical newness (*Neuzeit*) and the concomitant problem of political legitimacy.[33] If we do not take Koselleck's account to be authoritative history—if not taken as a truth correspondence theory of history, but rather as orthodox historiography that is indicative of the practice of the concept of crisis—we see how Koselleck's illustration sheds light on the various fault lines that have given rise to a form of political utopianism based on a discrepancy between immorality and innocence, or between what is thought to be contrived and what is taken as natural.

To better grasp the claim that political legitimacy issues from moral innocence, it is worth summarizing, albeit schematically, Koselleck's presentation of debates that raged over the course of the seventeenth and eighteenth centuries about the nature of natural law and moral law. For Koselleck, the early European debate over natural law and moral law centers on the seemingly unrelated questions of the subordination of action to conscience, on the one hand, and the permanent state of religious warfare, on the other. Hobbes in particular addresses these two subjects, arguing that, regardless of the good intentions of the various Christian communities, their respective claims to exclusiveness and the "subjective plurality" of the "authority of conscience" inevitably lead to civil war. Appeals to conscience, taken as private, subjective opinion, are the source of strife; they do not guarantee peace even when that opinion is motivated by the highest good of peace. For Hobbes, as is well known, peace requires a sovereign who is not subject to private conscience. Koselleck takes pains to underscore Hobbes's historical starting point: civil war. The call for the state was a call for the end of civil wars, not a call for progress;

a rationally derived destiny was not man's historical destiny because, for Hobbes, history was the history of sectarian warfare.[34] Peace was not equated with progress; rather the concern for peace was the context in which *faith in moral progress* developed.[35]

Koselleck's contention is that while Hobbes insists upon the necessity of politics for peace, he sets the distinction between morality and politics at the heart of absolutism.[36] The substance or content of the law does not establish its legality; instead, only formal legality itself is the rational basis for political obedience and peace, making political morality a matter of obeying *raison d'état*, or the strict validity of formal law. The move from the realm of private beliefs to public authority obtains through the social contract. Koselleck (1988, 31) comments, "The public interest, about which the sovereign alone has the right to decide, no longer lies in the jurisdiction of conscience. Conscience, which becomes alienated from the State, turns into private morality."[37] This notion of *a private inner space as the natural site* for the formulation of critique—the all-too-familiar moral or ethical subject—is what he refers to as the "apolitical politics" of the Enlightenment.

Koselleck moves forward in fairly linear fashion to note that, when the very possibility of differentiating between civil and private religion is questioned, most significantly, for instance, by Locke, the then-novel notion of "civil conscience" is given value.[38] Subjective opinion, described as having the character of laws (moral law, as opposed to divine or civil law), becomes the standard for judgment of both oneself and others. Citizens, not sovereigns, establish moral law via their judgments; and the legality of such law is likewise a matter of pure judgment.[39] Contrary to Hobbes, for whom there is a fundamental distinction between the private and public realms, Locke proposes that the public realm is constituted by the private realm. What is at stake is not the substance of the law, which was dictated by God and nature, but the validity of the law, which was subject to evaluation through reason and thus to judgment by bourgeois society. "Moral turns of mind are . . . interpreted by [Locke] in their social function— but not in order to deduce the State, as Hobbes had done, but to turn them into *constant acts of judgement* by the rising society" (Koselleck 1988, 57, my emphasis).

Koselleck traces the politicization of these debates, especially through the Masonic lodges and Bayle's Republic of Letters in France, to show how they involved utopian ideologies. For Bayle, the seventeenth-century skeptic known for his theorizations of the egalitarian Republic of Letters, reason, as the basis for judgment, was distinct from theology and revelation. He argued, for instance, that textual analysis entailed the systematic and persistent demand for reasons such that errors could be exposed or revealed, which of course implies that what is established on the grounds of reason is always subject to falsification as an error in judgment. Falsification, as a function of reason, constitutes an ever-present horizon, such that the very reliability of reason is constantly assailed, making reason by and large a matter of faith.[40]

The triumph of reason through the pure authority of private verdicts over both politics and the state entails a notion of historical progress that is necessarily a form of moral progress posing the ultimate challenge of emancipation. Self-rule, as an ethical principle, is generalized as a public, political demand, based on the assumption that "inner freedom" is realized in the external world. This principle amounts to the plainly incongruous demand for "a complete and total liberation of human beings from human rule" (Koselleck 2002, 250). What would be the burden of proof for such a demand? Koselleck notes that this burden of proof, as produced through reason, would have to be free of logical self-contradiction. By the end of the eighteenth century, the grounds for such proof had shifted from natural law to the historical future: "The transformation from personal rule into rational custodianship may be empirically demonstrated: such an expected, contested, and anticipated liberation of human beings from human subordination, in other words, their *redemption within history* or the negation of alienation" (2002, my emphasis). This European challenge, he argues, became a world historical challenge.[41]

Koselleck's (doubtless evident to my contemporaries) general point is that political utopianism entails a philosophy of history: the morally just and rational planning of history coincides in a hoped-for future, and the achievement of that future requires an interpretation of the relationship of the present to the past. He asks, as noted in the previous section of this chapter, what history itself might be, if it is established from the distance of time. And he replies that it is a matter of a *moral demand for a difference between the past and the future* (Koselleck 1988, 98–137; 2002, 110–44). If history comes to be defined as "where time itself occurs," or "in the relationship between past and future, which always constitutes an elusive present," the correlation between experience and expectation is necessarily transformed. Koselleck (2002, 111–12) clarifies this transformation via two problematic but generally accepted examples of historical modes of prognosis: "Until the early modern period, it was a general principle derived from experience that the future could bring nothing fundamentally new. Until the expected end of the world, sinful human beings (as seen from a Christian perspective) would not change; until then, the nature of man (as seen from a humanist perspective) would remain the same. For that reason, it was possible to issue prognoses, because the factors of human action or the naturally possible forms of government (as seen from an Aristotelian viewpoint) remained fundamentally the same." However, he concludes, "a prognosis that in principle expects the same as what has always been possible so far is no real prognosis at all." Koselleck (112–13) notes that Kant, as an exemplar, "assumes that the future will be different from the past because it is supposed to be different" and that this expectation is ultimately "a moral demand for a difference between past and future."

Regardless of whether or not this is a veritable empirical accounting of the past—whether or not the so-called pre- and early moderns truly expected nothing whatsoever from the future—this notion of *a radical temporal distinction* that engenders and is even necessary to transformation is a fundamental postulate for both historiography and for the notion of effective critique.[42] This demand for a temporal difference can be described in terms of a notion of progress as a moral task; and it is based on an alleged discrepancy between scientific or technological progress, on the one hand, and the moral positioning of human beings, on the other; or between honorable social emancipation and suspicious economic or political technologies. Morality must respond and constantly adapt to the exigencies of knowledge; it is posited as always insufficient or inadequate.[43] This discrepancy between morality and knowledge is taken to be an aporia, and it is signified by the term "crisis." And this signification refers to the formal, or logical, possibility of crisis, as found in the thought of Aristotle, Hegel, and Marx. In the expectation of temporal difference, it implies or entails an ethical imperative, be that explicit or not.[44]

For Koselleck, political utopianism as a philosophy of history—or the positing of a transcendent that accommodates the idea that humanity can devise its own destiny—actually produces "crisis," and it does so in two ways.[45] First, it is a philosophy of history that allows one to posit the very possibility of a "break" with the past. His central thesis is that, with the French Revolution, the conviction that conclusions about the past are necessary to an understanding of the future is challenged by the idea that the future is to be apprehended as indiscernible. The Revolution thus represents "the crisis of the Enlightenment," or a new mode of consciousness of *history as crisis*.[46] Second, and equally novel, is the practical mode of social action that this historical consciousness entails: one can act "on" history to transform it, which, for Koselleck, denotes a distinctly modern way of postulating the relationship between theory and practice.[47]

The concept of critique, as understood by the end of the eighteenth century—that is, not as criticism of the state or of political policy, but as a judgment of the *validity* of institutions and concepts themselves—informs this manner of understanding the relationship between theory and practice. As a universal standard of judgment, through the exercise of reason to resolve historical contingency, critique engendered what Koselleck sees as a form of "hypocrisy" because the depiction of political crisis as the *logical outcome* of historical progress obscures the *contingent political* significance of such critique.[48] Hypocrisy lies in the simultaneous "critique of all power" and yet the desire to achieve "the power to judge all mankind" (Edwards 2006, 438). In that sense, perpetual critique—of oneself via moral conscience and of the world against a standard of reason—is coterminous with a perpetual state of crisis. Critique makes the future "a maelstrom," says

Koselleck (1988, 109), astutely. "If criticism is the ostensible resting point of human thought, then thought becomes a restless exercise in movement" (108). In other words, the constant quest to authenticate the supreme authority of reason transpires through the perpetual process of critique, which entails infinite renewal and is based on the idea of duty toward the future and motivated by faith in the yet-to-be-discovered truth.

To summarize, in his demonstration of the mutual constitution of the cognate concepts, critique and crisis, Koselleck apprehends the Enlightenment not as a sociopolitical organization but rather as an ethos that formed around key concepts, such as "state," "society," "politics," "morality." This formation depended fundamentally on the temporalization of history, for which the concept of crisis was crucial. For Koselleck, by the eighteenth century, "crisis" denoted a freestanding, primarily historical concept. Its emergence as such was concurrent with the gradual establishment of "history" as a discipline—or with the practice of political and social history as the diagnosis of time. Effectively, Reinhart Koselleck provides a remarkable inquiry into the process of temporalization and the metaphysics of history.[49]

But then one can ask, whose history? and what history? Koselleck's account clearly serves the self-narration or self-constitution of "modernity" as (sovereign) History. And, alongside the question of "other people's" histories, or other histories, is the issue of taking myriad ontic possibilities into account, of displacing humanist or human-centric history. As Kathleen Davis maintains regarding such narration and its attendant practice of periodization, "the paradox of a self-constituting modernity is folded into the cut of periodization itself, and the 'modern' can emerge as unproblematically sovereign" (2008, 87). This is an iteration of the claim I make herein about the term "crisis." Similarly to Kathleen Davis, I take Koselleck's work to be "both an example of and a factor in critical theory's difficulty with addressing, and sometimes even recognizing, events that defy preconceived concepts of religion, secularism, democracy, and politics" (2008, 87, and 5–6). However, not being preoccupied with so-called modernity or the problem of secularization and its constitutive terms, I do not dwell on the concepts of religion, democracy, and politics. Instead, I raise a question that is crucially related to her characterization of Koselleck's method and narrative, though with my sites trained on the term "crisis": what counts as an event? I likewise take up the dilemma of critical theory, though only insofar as "critique" is the cognate of crisis, to which I turn below. As we shall see, and as Koselleck has made clear, crisis invokes a moral demand for a difference between the past and the future. Critical historical consciousness— or the specific, historical way of knowing the world as "history"— discerns historical significance in terms of ethical failures: what went wrong?[50]

THE TEST

With reason as our judge, we are consumed with the problem of establishing the validity of claims to social or political critique, which makes both moral righteousness and faith in deliverance the uncertain terms of our historical self-consciousness. Of course, the grounds for human progress have been an object of suspicion for several centuries. Historical narratives produced by "Enlightenment rationalists" themselves displayed the form of irony associated with a self-conscious, self-critical awareness and an ethics of skepticism (see Burke 1969; White 1973).[51] And by the end of the nineteenth century, despite faith in technological progress, the search for general causes in history, or a philosophy of history, was deemed by many a forsaken enterprise. The very notion of historical progress and pretensions to a science of history generally were abandoned, especially after the scourge of the First World War.[52] But what is obscured in denunciations of the notion of historical progress and the disavowal of non-contingent grounds for judgment is the way in which the temporal understanding of action and history, or theory and practice, remains contingent upon the concept of crisis. The concept of crisis is bound to its cognate "critique" and is established, as a concept, through the very widespread but strange idea that history could be alienated in terms of its philosophy—that is, that one could perceive a dissonance between historical events and representations of those events.

One might suppose that contemporary modes of critique take into account the problem of assuming a dissonance between history and a philosophy of history, or even simply between history and morality. Since the time of the differentiation of reason as a category of history, ostensibly initiated during the eighteenth century, reason itself has been posited as a problem: reason cannot claim a position from which to transcend history, or an Archimedean point of observation and validation; it is a wholly contingent mode of observation and yet it is taken to be the ultimate means to overcoming the condition of contingency. The centrality of this dilemma is evident through centuries of debate over the possibility of a legitimate or valid place of criticism, of the critic, and of critique. Criticism operates through judgment, making the critic somehow distant or even apparently autonomous from social practice. Or, in denial of judgment as a feasible or defensible operation, critique is taken to be praxis, or a form of practice. Debates about these positions run through the legendary work of scholars associated with the Institute for Social Research, or the Frankfurt School, who sought to secure the grounds for immanent critique, or non-foundationalist grounds for political action. Ultimately, whether judgment or praxis, immanent critique takes as its object the discrepancy between how things are, on the one hand, and how they ought to be or how they could be, on the other (see, for example, Adorno 1973; Horkheimer 1974; Habermas 1984–87).[53]

Habermas (1984–87, 1987, 1982), for instance, maintains that, without a theory of history, there can be no immanent critique. In order to secure the normative foundations of critique, where norms are universally valid and binding statements, one must elaborate normatively justified goals—how things ought to be. Because the contingency of immanence is paralyzing, it must be transcended via formal structures of rationality, which can be related to historically or culturally situated (linguistic) reason.[54] For Habermas, the very critique of reason, which demonstrates that there are no epistemological or philosophical foundations for securing rationality beyond its contingent or partial manifestation, is itself a rational critique, or "performative contradiction" arising from self-referentiality. Thus the problem of self-grounding, or the legitimation of theories in terms of the very distinctions (e.g., rational versus irrational) that permit their elaboration, leads to infinite regress. This dilemma of self-grounding and legitimation is what Habermas takes to be the "crisis of modernity." In keeping with a long-standing tradition of critical theory, or analyses of the generalization of instrumental reason and modes of domination inherent to late capitalism, his scholarship is defined by the problem of meaning ("lost meaning") and alienation. The object of critique is a distorted pattern of historical development. The crisis of modernity signifies the discrepancy between the world and what the world ought to be, as well as the problem of securing the grounds for such critique.

And this disquiet over the grounds for knowledge of this discrepancy persists in the work of contemporary scholars, navigating in the wake of critical theory and the unshakable, impossible question, what is critique? In reply to that very question, Judith Butler, in a reflection on Michel Foucault's writing, says: "Critique is always a critique of some instituted practice, discourse, episteme, institution, and it loses its character the moment in which it is abstracted from its operation and made to stand alone as a purely generalizable practice. But if this is true, this does not mean that no generalizations are possible or that, indeed, we are mired in particularisms. On the contrary, we tread here in an area of constrained generality, one which broaches the philosophical, but must, if it is to remain critical, remain at a distance from that very achievement" (2002, 212).[55] For Butler—following Foucault's own grappling with the unshakable, impossible "What is critique?" (the title of an essay he delivered in 1978, himself revisiting the labors of Kant's 1784 text, "Was ist Aufklärung?" ["What Is the Enlightenment?"])[56]—critique entails suspension of judgment; and it "offers a new practice of values based on that very suspension" (2002, 212). This suspension of judgment means that "the primary task of critique will not be to evaluate whether its objects—social conditions, practices, forms of knowledge, power, and discourse—are good or bad, valued highly or demeaned, but to bring into relief the very framework of evaluation itself" (2002, 214, and cf. Foucault 1997a, 59). A critical relation to norms inheres in a reflexive relationship to modes of categorization and the forms of rationality that organize and give sense and significance to practice (Foucault 1997b, 315–17). Thus, although this practice of critique elides the judgment between the way the world is, on the one hand, and the way the world ought to be, on the other, it reiterates a Kantian conception of critique as an operation for ascertaining and revealing the limits of reason—though this is achieved not through a transcendental deduction, but by seeking the limits of knowledge (Foucault 1997b, 315).[57] But why seek the limits of knowledge? Not just for pure transgression, as Butler explains: "One does not drive to the limits for a thrill experience, or because limits are dangerous and sexy, or because it brings us into a titillating proximity with evil. One asks about the limits of ways of knowing because one has *already run up against a crisis* within the epistemological field in which one lives" (215, my emphasis). This is a "tear in the fabric of our epistemological web," the "discursive impasse from which the necessity and urgency of critique emerges" (215)—Koselleck's rupture, *the a priori of the event*, "a means for a future" (Foucault 1997a, 42).

So when the grounds for critical reason are deserted for the even more unstable lands of partial and local truths, crisis is not solved. To the contrary, the concept of crisis becomes a prime mover in poststructuralist thought: while truth cannot be secured, it is nonetheless performed in moments of crisis, when the grounds for truth claims are supposedly made bare and the limits of intelligibility are potentially subverted or transgressed. Thus, for example, epistemological crisis is defined by Judith Butler (tautologically?) as a "crisis over what constitutes the limits of intelligibility" (1993, 138). Many academic authors, including myself (Roitman 2005), take crisis to be the starting point for narration.[58] Inspired by the work of Foucault, we assume that if we start with the disciplinary concepts or techniques that allow us to think ourselves as subjects—that enable us to tell the truth about ourselves—then limits to ways of knowing necessarily entail epistemological crises.[59] For Butler, then, subject formation transpires through crisis: that is, crisis, or the disclosure of epistemological limits, occasions critique, and potentially gives rise to counter-normativities that speak the unspeakable (1999, 2004, 307–8; and see Boland 2007). For Foucault, crisis signifies a discursive impasse and the potential for a new form of historical subject.

For both, crisis is productive; it is the means to transgress and is necessary for change or transformation. In keeping with this, because reason has no end other than itself, the decisive duty of critique is essentially to produce crisis—to engage in the permanent critique of one's self "through a practice of knowledge that is foreign to one's own." To be in critical relation to normative life is a form of ethics and a virtue (Foucault 1985, 1997a, 1997b, 303–19). In the words of Simon Critchley, who sees crisis as necessary for politics, or for producing a "critical consciousness of the present," philosophy would have no purpose in a world without crisis: "the real crisis would be a situation where crisis was not recognized" (1999, 12). If the grounds for truth are necessarily contingent or partial, and if philosophy thus has no intrinsic object, its authority only possibly emerges as such in moments of crisis, which are defined as the "time when philosophy happens."[60]

Meaning, significance, and truth are of course problems—it seems that they constitute our condition of crisis and are addressed by reflection on the possibility for critique.[61] But this category of crisis, so integral to the production of new forms and the very intelligibility of the subject, is never problematized despite its cognate and historical-semantic relationship to critique. Apparently, for scholars past and present, attention to the problem of the grounds for critique has eclipsed the seemingly less imperative question of the grounds for positing crisis. The imperative to critique or even to sustain a critical relation to normativity ironically risks ontologizing the category of crisis. This is curious: Why should crisis, as a category, be so self-evident? How is it that the grounds for critique became the defining problem of epistemology while the grounds for thinking the human condition in terms of crisis did not?[62] Although I cannot answer such a very broad question, it is worth noting that its effects are with us today. Indeed, even for those who renounce the possibility and duty of critique, crisis is self-evident. Thus the very first section of Bruno Latour's influential book *We Have Never Been Modern* (1993) is entitled "Crisis," referring to "the crisis of the critical stance" but never problematizing the very grounds for the concept of crisis. One might conjecture: if modernity has never obtained, then crisis has not either.

Unable to establish the noncontingent grounds from which to claim critique, truth is necessarily immanent and critique is consigned to the constant unveiling of latencies.[63] The latter have been characterized in terms of invisible relations, sediments of tradition, false consciousness, ideologies, subjectivization, naturalized categories, or normalization. Even when the criterion for truth is no longer defined in terms of the logic of noncontradiction, or internal consistency, critique is thought to occur through paradox: through the purging of contradiction and paradox; through the commitment to obstinately demonstrate the paradox of power, or the necessary exclusions (the Other, non-sovereigns) that expose the foundations of power to be contingent suppositions; or through the confidence that paradox is a manifestation of conditions of crisis, and hence for critique and transformation, thus seemingly resolving or at least provisionally settling conditions of paradox . . .

If by paradox, we mean "a permissible and meaningful statement that leads nonetheless to antinomies or undecidability (or, more strictly, a demonstrable proposition that has such consequences)" (Luhmann 2002, 142), then an ample conceptual history or, better, genealogy of the concept of crisis would account for the antinomies, or how crisis has come to be a manner of signifying such a state of affairs.[64] A paradox that is said to be an antimony "produces a self contradiction by accepted ways of reasoning. It establishes that some tacit and trusted pattern of reasoning must be made explicit and henceforward be avoided or revised" (Quine 1966, 5). This kind of paradox "brings on the crises in thought" (5). And such crises are seen to be the bases for critique. When faced with two equally valid or persuasive propositions, which are irreducible the one to the other, critique is elaborated in the disjuncture between "is" and "ought" or between "is" and "could be."[65] This disjuncture denotes the formal possibility of crisis: the contradiction that drives dialectical methods typical to social science narrative (Marx and Hegel being the obvious examples) as well as the dichotomies (subject/object, theory/practice, validity/value, intelligible/empirical, transcendence/immanence) that are at the foundation of all social theory and social science narration.[66] The paradox at hand is best described as that established between the invariance of logical truth and the constitutive mutability of our experience of that truth. And because we can only observe or differentiate—that is, produce these very dichotomies—from within immanence, we effectively assume a negative occupation of the immanent world (Fuchs 1989, 24, cited by Rasch 2000, 109; and see Luhmann [1992] 1998; Deleuze and Guattari 1996, 35–60).[67]

This self-referential or nonempirical moment of empirical knowledge (rejected by Quine, the empiricist) does not deny the existence of an external world or order of being, nor does it indicate pure self-reference or the inaccessibility of that world/order: "There is an external world . . . but we have no direct contact with it. Without knowing, cognition could not reach the external world. In other words, knowing is only a self-referential process. Knowledge can only know itself, although it can—as if out of the corner of its eye—determine that this is only possible if there is more than only cognition. Cognition deals with an external world that remains unknown and has to, as a result, come to see that it cannot see what it cannot see" (Luhmann 1990a, 64–65).[68] Without delving unnecessarily into Luhmann's theory of knowledge, it is important to note that his approach is situated "beyond realism and constructivism": "Concepts are not empirical theories and, hence, cannot be true or false. They constitute the language in which we formulate empirical statements (about the degree of inflation) and substantive theories that are either causal (about the causes and effects of inflation), or functional in nature (about the functions of inflation, i.e., about the problems solved by inflation). Conceptual frameworks constitute . . . the non-empirical (intensional, grammatical or self-referential) aspect of empirical theories" (Christis 2001, 345).[69] Concepts originate not in the structure of experience of a Kantian transcendental subject, or in the knowing subject, but rather in observing systems, or empirical "epistemic subjects," which are interfaces between biological, psychic, or social systems and environments.[70] There is no transcendental point of departure for Luhmann; there are only self-referential systems.

Without a correspondence between knowledge and the external world or order of things, Luhmann posits the concept of observation as a means of designation via distinctions. A first observation (money) requires a prior distinction (money/not money), which can only be the object of a second-order observation. As Luhmann has demonstrated consistently, this is not a matter of empirical observations, but rather *a matter of logical observations*, which are distinctions and which are meaning-constituting. *Crisis is just one distinction.* It is a postulate that brings a descriptive situation "under conceptual control" (Luhmann, 2002, 38).[71] This basic operation allows some thing to become distinct and hence intelligible—the observation gives rise to a form, and thus meaning (Luhmann [1992] 1998, 46–55). Significantly, the concept of observation or distinction does not proceed from binaries or oppositions. For example, my claim is that it cannot be the case that there is crisis/noncrisis, which then permits observations. Rather "crisis" is a distinction that transcends oppositions between knowledge and experience, or subject and object; it is a distinction that generates meaning precisely because it contains its own self-reference.[72] As Luhmann says, "What can be distinguished by means of these distinctions will become 'information'" (1990b, 131). That is to say, from my point of view, the term "crisis" establishes second-order observation; it is not an object of first-order observation.[73] Crisis is a means to externalize self-reference. This external reference for judgment in a necessarily self-referential system—or a distinction that generates and refers to an "inviolate level" of order (not crisis)—is seen to be contingent (historical crises) and yet is likewise posited as beyond the play of contingency, being a logical necessity that is affirmed in paradox (the formal possibility of crisis).[74]

Without doing justice to the depths of Luhmann's work, suffice it to underscore the point that, in a world that is posited as an immanent field of observations, one is necessarily in a self-referential system, which is unavoidably paradoxical (Luhmann 1990b, 123–43; 1995, 56–57; 1998; 2002, 130–33; Deleuze 1994). In other words, if we take ourselves to be without a position from which to observe society in its totality, there can be no universal principles, but only self-referential principles, which are paradoxical.[75] What Luhmann communicates to us is that such self-referential paradoxes are unavoidable, and there is no cause to prohibit or avoid them. Habitually posited as a logical contradiction, paradox is a foundational sign for an order without an origin. This means, as he says, that "all knowledge and all action have to be founded on paradoxes and not on principles; on the self-referential unity of the positive and the negative—that is, on an ontologically unqualifiable world" (Luhmann 2002, 101; see also 86–87 and 142–43). Without recognition of these conditions of paradox, standards for evaluating social conditions produce descriptions and judgments in terms of pathology—that is, *as deficient but not as merely paradoxical* (cf. Luhmann 1990b, 136–37).[76]

Crisis is a blind spot that enables the production of knowledge.[77] It is a distinction that, perhaps as least since the late eighteenth century, and like all latencies, is not seen as simply paradox, but rather as an error or deformation—a discrepancy between the world and knowledge of the world. But if we take crisis to be a blind spot, or a distinction, which makes certain things visible and others invisible, it is merely an a priori. Crisis is claimed, but it remains a latency; it is never itself explained because it is necessarily further reduced to other elements, such as capitalism, economy, neoliberalism, finance, politics, culture, subjectivity.[78] In that sense, crisis is not a condition to be observed (loss of meaning, alienation, faulty knowledge); it is an observation that produces meaning. More precisely, it is a distinction that secures "a world" for observation or, in Obama's terms, it secures the grounds for witnessing and testing.[79]

CHAPTER 2

CRISIS NARRATIVES

BUBBLES

Crisis is an observation that produces meaning. What are the consequences of this proposition? If crisis is necessary to the elaboration
of critique, why take the trouble to displace its foundational status in
social science narratives? The first answer is simple: when crisis is
posited as the very condition of contemporary situations, certain questions become possible while others are foreclosed. What questions,
then, were foreclosed by the immediate qualification of the state of the
subprime mortgage market in 2007–9 and the inaugural state of the
union in 2009 as states of crisis? We must consider, also, what forms
of critique these crisis narratives engender—critique and crisis being
cognates. These forms of critique entail assumptions about how categories like "the market" or "finance" *should* function and consequential
conjecture about how deviations from "true" market or financial value
were produced. They cannot account for the ways that such value is
produced in the first place. In other words, when crisis is posited as an
a priori, it obviates such accounts of positive or practical knowledge.
It follows that the second answer is more difficult to entertain insofar
as it causes us to consider what narratives are precluded by the crisis
narrative, or the post hoc judgment of deviation, of failure. What are
at stake are not only possible stories about the world, but also worlds.[1]

*

Barack Obama's inaugural crisis, where we began this book, takes as its referent the subprime mortgage market and related financial markets in collateralized debt obligations, credit default swaps, and collateralized loan obligations, among other financial products and their associated trade. The dizzying array of crisis narratives that immediately overdetermined the significance of events—now a veritable "canon of crisis analysis" (Braithwaite 2011)—all proceed from the question, what went wrong?[2] These narratives are structured in terms of a quest for the "roots," "origins," and "causes" of the crisis; none hesitate over the matter of positing the term "crisis" itself. All are concerned to unearth the history from which we have become alienated: they hope to reveal the "secret origin" (Lewis 2010, 1), the "deeper causes" (Skidelsky 2009, 4), the "underlying contradictions" (Harvey 2011, 89), the "hidden history" (McLean and Nocera 2010)— all of which have led to distortions or deviations from a proper or more correct historical progression. Moreover, these narrations, in their claim to reveal moments of alienation likewise claim to "reveal history" itself (Shiller 2008).

The origins, causes, and hidden agents of this history are defined by an array of interrelated terms: liquidity, asset bubble, credit, interest rates, deregulation, speculation, corruption, fraud, traders, Quants, the Fed, ratings agencies, regulators, finance capital, fictive capital, virtual economy, innovation, systemic risk, asset pricing, failed price-discovery mechanism, political and economic policy, ideology, neoliberalism, economic theory, originate-to-distribute practice, mathematical models, derivatives, shareholder value, financialization, risk management, regulatory capture, overproduction, underconsumption, over-accumulation, and the falling rate of profit (for examples, see Arrighi and Silver 1999; Bookstaber 2007; Taleb 2007; Cooper 2008; Morris 2008; Shiller 2008; Turner 2008; Akerlof and Shiller 2009; Cohan 2009; Foster and Magdoff 2009; Fox 2009; Krugman 2009; Lordon 2009; McDonald 2009; Reinhart and Rogoff 2009; Skidelsky 2009; Sorkin 2009; Tett 2009; Zuckerman 2009; Gorton 2010; Greenspan 2010; Grossberg 2010; Harvey 2010; Johnson and Kwak 2010; Lewis 2010; McLean and Nocera 2010; Roubini and Mihm 2010; Stiglitz 2010; Touraine 2010; Krippner 2011; Balibar 2012).³ Ultimately the question of blame, be that in the form of moral or technical failure, provides closure and hence the possibility for rectification, emancipation, redemption.

If one distills the contemporary canon of crisis analysis down to the central debates, we find that what is at issue in this recent canon of crisis narratives is the problem of liquidity in either the banking system or in the capitalist world system, depending on one's theoretical approach. The three main modes of interpretation—the defense of efficient markets, the neo-Keynesian critique of the efficient market hypothesis, and the Marxist-inspired critique of the world capitalist system—are structured by three distinct problems, respectively: pricing assets, regulating so-called asset bubbles, and financing the ever-expanding logics of capitalism. Without entering into the details of those interpretations, which are reviewed amply in the books cited above, the narratives resulting from these approaches all attempt to document a differential between the "real economy," on the one hand, and a "fictive" or "overvalued" state of affairs, which is seemingly immaterial, on the other. The crisis is given a measure, be it a decline in real GDP ("negative growth") or the falling rate of profit, again depending on the theoretical approach. What is needed, or hoped for, is a return to what might be deemed real value—to true prices, to underlying fundamentals, to material production.

In the prevailing, generic crisis narrative, this "real economy" is represented by houses.⁴ No matter the spiraling details of finance gone amuck, in the standard narrative of the 2007–9 financial crisis, the precipitous historical event is the decline in housing prices, which happens naturally. In his wonderful tribute to Maynard Keynes, Robert Skidelsky (2009, 4) offers what could now be described as the authoritative "thumbnail sketch" of the crisis:

> A global inverted pyramid of household and bank debt was built on a narrow range of underlying assets—American house prices. When they started to fall, the debt balloon started to deflate, at first slowly, ultimately with devastating speed. Many of the bank loans had been made to "subprime" mortgage borrowers—borrowers with poor prospects of repayment. Securities based on sub-prime

debt entered the balance sheets of banks all round the world. When house prices started to fall, the banks suddenly found these securities falling in value; fearing insolvency, with their investments impaired by an unknown amount, they stopped lending to each other and to their customers. This caused a "credit crunch."

When housing prices started to fall . . . Never accounted for in itself, the decline in housing prices is typically presented as a natural development: "In principle, the securities that combined many mortgages spread the risk. But much depended on the assumptions that housing prices would keep rising and defaults would be relatively few. When housing prices began to trend down, the mortgage-backed securities became toxic, and it was hard to sort out the good from the bad" (Calhoun 2011, 14; see also Shiller 2008 on "Bubble Trouble"). The downward trend in housing prices is assumed to be a natural result of a glut in supply, a development that is paired with the tendency for homeowners to default on their outstanding loans.

One version of the crisis narrative, penned by David Harvey and best characterized as "historical-geographical materialism," does give a contingent reason for this alleged natural trend downward in housing prices. He writes (2010, 1–2):

It was only in mid-2007, when the foreclosure wave hit the white middle class in hitherto booming and significantly Republican urban and suburban areas in the US south (particularly Florida) and west (California, Arizona and Nevada), that officialdom started to take note and the mainstream press began to comment. New condominium and housing tract development (often in "bedroom communities" or across peripheral urban zones) began to be affected. By the end of 2007, nearly 2 million people had lost their homes and 4 million more were thought to be in danger of foreclosure. Housing values plummeted almost everywhere across the US and many households found themselves owing more on their houses than they were worth. This set in motion a downward spiral of foreclosures that depressed housing values even further.

Foreclosures, and *then* a contraction in the value of houses.

From a fundamentally different perspective, Robert Shiller, the well-known liberal economist, writes (2008, 7):

> High home prices made it profitable to build homes, and the share of residential investment in U.S. gross domestic product (GDP) rose to 6.3% in the fourth quarter of 2005, the highest level since the pre–Korean War housing boom of 1950–51. The huge supply of new homes began to glut the market, and, despite the optimistic outlooks of national leaders, U.S. home prices began to fall in mid-2006. As prices declined at an accelerating rate, the boom in home construction collapsed.
>
> At the same time, mortgage rates began to reset to higher levels after initial "teaser" periods ended. Borrowers, particularly sub-prime borrowers, began defaulting, often owing more than their homes were worth or unable to support their higher monthly payments with current incomes.

At the same time, mortgage rates began to reset . . . borrowers . . . began defaulting.

As Harvey and virtually all other narrators of the 2007–9 property-market decline claim, the creation of an extensive, global credit market (or debt market) allowed for (or produced) the very high valuation of housing. Robert Brenner, David Harvey, and Giovanni Arrighi, all writing from a Marxist-inspired approach to a total history of capital, provide detailed illustrations of chronic overcapacity, repressed wages and thus insufficient demand, and material expansion followed by financial expansion so as to account for the troubles in the property and housing markets.[5] Harvey (2010, 17) thus exclaims, "The demand problem was temporarily bridged with respect to housing by debt-financing the developers as well as the buyers. The financial institutions collectively controlled both the supply of, and demand for, housing!"

The manufacture and selling of debt, and not just houses, has been the most remarkable growth industry of the past decade, or more.[6] Of course, this point is not lost on the canon of crisis analyses of all theoretical and ideological persuasions. Skidelsky, the neo-Keynesian, notes (2009, 14): "The manufacture and selling of debt by the City of London has been the major British growth industry of the last ten years, far outstripping the growth of all real assets except housing and all services except hairdressing." This situation is obviously not limited to the City of London, barring perhaps the lead in hairstyling. Harvey (2003, 112–13), in his explanation of how the problem of over-accumulation in the capitalist world system is "solved" via a "spatial fix," says, "In a curious backwash effect, we find that some 20 per cent of GDP growth in the United States in 2002 was attributable to consumers refinancing their mortgage debt on the inflated values of their housing and using the extra money they gained for immediate consumption (in effect, mopping up overaccumulating capital in the primary circuit)."

For liberal economists, neo-Keynesians, and neo-Marxists, crisis emerges from a chasm between "the real," on the one hand, and what is qualified respectively as an illogical departure from the real, a sub-stitute for "the real," or purely fictitious, on the other. In all cases, we have the story of our alienation. In an admittedly extremely sche-matic staging of this alienation story, we can say that liberal econo-mists (Greenspan, Merton, Samuelson, Scholes, Shiller) assume logi-cal linkages between a self-correcting pricing mechanism and the optimal allocation of resources; to a deviation in the relationship be-tween credit and collateral, or the mispricing of assets and/or risk; to departures from the underlying fundamentals, all of which raise the problem of erroneous value. Neo-Keynesians (Cooper, Duncan, Krugman, Roubini and Mihm, Stiglitz) set up a logical progression from the U.S. trade deficit or a trade imbalance, to a current accounts imbalance, to the printing of money or credit creation, all of which raise the problem of fiat money. For neo-Marxists (Arrighi, Brenner, Harvey, Wallerstein), the schematic and reduced logical progression is from chronic overcapacity or insufficient demand, to the falling rate of profit, to the expansion of the credit system or financializa-tion, all of which raise the problem of fictitious capital. For some, the overextension of credit impacted upon optimal price allocation, giving rise to a tide of exuberant speculation, and thus a dramatic rise in home prices; for others, a savings glut resulted in the poor allo-cation of capital, which led to the increase in home prices; for still others, the over-accumulation of capital led to the wrong allocation of resources to profitable private investment as opposed to wages, and hence the escalation of home prices. Either way, crisis is presented as both a logical and analogous form inherent to the telos of an economy. Either way, finance is the locus of our alienation from underlying value, the fundamentals, the gold standard, material production, use value, the real economy . . .[7] And either way, something went wrong.

Joshua Clover (2011) takes note of the convergence between Marxist and non-Marxist narratives with a dash of irony and an appreciation, albeit undeveloped, of these accounts as narrative forms.[8]

> An era of industrial expansion and real growth bears the seeds of its own undoing; when it fails, the financial sector must leap in to generate profits elsewhere. But these expansions of the financial sector are always temporary, if not indeed illusory. There is no financial expansion that is not a bubble. Credit is, for all the many mysteries and wonders in which it traffics, money spent now for work to be done later: a mortgage, a share of IBM, and the mezzanine tranche of synthetic Collateralized Debt Obligation are all, in more or less evident ways, "claims on future labor." The moment that it becomes evident that all that productive labor is not waiting up around the bend, then nobody wants to give out any more credit. And the creditors want their money. And the investors want out of risk. Pop.

Clover's irony only goes so far: he accepts the notion that finance is illusory. The bubble is a metaphor for the dissonance between empirical history, on the one hand, and a philosophy of history, on the other—between truly grounded material value and unmoored, theoretical, speculative assessments.

HOUSES

Let us return to houses. Consider the two statements I underscored, as a minimalist subtext, above:

"Foreclosures, and *then* a contraction in the value of houses."

"*At the same time,* mortgage rates began to reset . . . borrowers . . . began defaulting."

Of course, mortgage rates did not reset. To be more precise, financial models were designed; standards and measures were assumed, manipulated, and performed; analyses were implemented and translated; interpretations were formulated, adapted, and communicated; scenarios were deployed; possible outcomes were debated; and rate operations were structured into mortgage agreements, such that, at a certain point, they were qualified as "floating." Likewise, foreclosures did not happen; homeowners were foreclosed upon. The natural tendency for housing prices to trend downward—the founding event of the crisis narrative—is less naturalized history than a set of distinct designs, decisions, determinations, and contexts.

Ultimately, the question then arises: when does a credit (asset) become a debt (toxic asset)—how do we demarcate the first form from the second?[9] At what point do houses figured as equity become figured as debt? At what point do subprime mortgage bonds transform from an asset to a liability? The answers to those questions serve to denaturalize crisis narratives.[10] Given that the creation of an extensive debt market, or the leveraging of the assets and consumer markets as well as the banking system, took place over a significant period of time; given the widespread practice of debt-financed asset pricing, which was pursued over a significant period of time; and given that many individual and institutional actors were shorting the market, or betting on default, over a significant period of time—when does the judgment of crisis obtain? How do we come to see default, which is a daily, mundane occurrence, as truly exceptional? That is, when and how is it marked as a sign of crisis? Why crisis now?[11]

The most common answer, with respect to the subprime mortgage market in the years 2007–9, is that crisis obtained when there was literally "no market," when interbank loans failed to occur, when there was literally no liquidity, or no agreement on value. According to this view, for instance, the assumption that an asset can be sold to repay a loan does not hold at a macro level because "if one million houses are sold at the same time prices will crash and the entire housing market will *become* under-collateralised" (Cooper 2008, 115, my emphasis). But if we take the "entire housing market" to include all financial products and instruments associated with the subprime mortgage market and secondary markets, noting that they are part of integrated capital markets, then we can surmise that the United States housing market was *always, already* under-collateralized.

What *exactly* is in crisis? As this exploration of current crisis narratives makes clear, answers to that question inevitably have recourse to a secular prime mover, be it capitalism, financialization, neoliberalism, deregulation, the business cycle, systemic risk, et cetera. The hasty assumption that some thing is in crisis induces an inevitable leap to abstraction because, as I indicated above, crisis, in itself, cannot be located or observed as an object of first-order knowledge. One can make the statement "I lost a million dollars" as a first-order observation; but the declaration "This is a crisis" is necessarily a second-order observation. Therefore, in our crisis haste, we completely bypass certain crucial, interrelated questions, such as: How did debt come to figure as an asset class? *And how is the claim to crisis, and our assent to crisis narratives, crucial to the re-transcription of assets into debts?* In order to entertain those questions, crisis cannot be taken as a description of a historical situation nor can it be taken to be a diagnosis of the status of history, as I argued at length above. If the claim to crisis is a distinction that produces information, then this claim is not a logical diagnosis of ontology ("crisis"), but rather a post hoc and necessarily political denunciation of a particular situation.[12]

Instead of taking as natural fact the assertion that housing prices trended downward, I would like to go down a hypothetical road, which is more of a conjecture than a counterargument or counternarrative: analyses were made and decisions were taken to initiate the transformation of debt via a massive devaluation, and housing prices dropped. Not the reverse. Here, instead of a financial crisis due to rampant, irrational speculation; instead of a systemic crisis of capitalism due to underlying contradictions; instead of a crisis of the banking system due to deregulation or mistaken policy; and instead of crisis qualified as faulty risk management due to defective financial models and erroneous forecasting, we have a particular (and thus political) solution to what is declared a problem for certain people. The point is not that there is a political conspiracy to be denounced: financial and political actors do not act with omnipotent voluntarism. And my aim is not to posit a more accurate account, to establish the true meaning of historical events. Rather, the conjecture, or thought experiment, I put forth regarding possible, alternative narratives about houses and their worth allows for consideration of what might constitute proof of crisis. The point is to consider what possible, alternative narratives might be generated without recourse to a sociology of error, without constructing a post hoc narrative of denunciation.

But, in the end, maybe houses are irrelevant. Contra the notion that housing prices plummeted, hence gluttonous consumers found their two-car-garage homes to be worthless digs, Michael Lewis, the overly popularized financial journalist, notes that because millions of homeowners could only repay mortgages if their homes rose dramatically in value, home prices did not need to plummet for default to occur; "they merely needed to stop rising at the unprecedented rates they had the previous years for a vast numbers of Americans to default on their home loans" (2010, 65). The journalist Paul Krugman, who dons academic credentials as an economist, likewise comments (2007): "The run-up of home prices made even less sense than the dot-com bubble—I mean, there wasn't even a glamorous new technology to justify claims that old rules no longer applied"—a remark that was never taken as more than an ironic aside. One wonders with respect to these influential analyses: instead of obsessing, after the fact, over the notion that home prices were wrong, or overvalued, one might have inquired into how home values were being determined.

Before turning to this latter point about valuation and the production of value, I first suggest an admittedly unorthodox reading of Lewis's book *The Big Short*, which tells a popular, novelistic story of corruption, complete with the bad guys and good guys of finance. Indeed, *The Big Short* was a nonfiction bestseller largely because it is the story of an outsider "good guy" hero, acting literally against all odds (he is shorting the market . . .) amidst his fellow bad guys of finance. However, if one looks past the simplistic moral of the story, some of what Lewis documents betrays the sleaze, instead chronicling the efficacy of highly leveraged markets and *the tremendous wealth they produced*:

The alacrity with which subprime borrowers paid off their loans was yet another strange aspect of this booming market. It had to do with the structure of the loans, which were fixed for two or three years at an artificially low teaser rate before shooting up to the "go-to" floating rate. "They were making loans to low-income people at a teaser rate when they knew they couldn't afford to pay the go-to rate," said Eisman [the hero, who reveals the moral]. "They were doing it so that when the borrowers get to the end of the teaser rate period, they'd have to refinance, so the lenders can make more money off them." Thirty-year loans were thus designed to be re-paid in a few years. At worst, if you bought credit default swaps on $100 million in subprime mortgage bonds you might wind up shelling out premium for six years—call it $12 million. At best: Losses on the loans rose from the current 4 percent to 8 percent, and you made $100 million. The bookies were offering you odds of somewhere between 6:1 and 10:1 when the odds of it working out felt more like 2:1. Anyone in the business of making smart bets couldn't not do it. (Lewis 2010, 65–66)

As most of us now know, credit default swaps are a form of insur-ance contract. Essentially serving as credit protection, these contracts are central to outright bets against the market, being agreements be-tween two or more parties that define the terms of payment in the event of default on a third party's bond. Homes are almost superflu-ous; the bet is on credit risk, or on the price of credit risk. The irrele-vance of houses is driven home by Lewis's claim—which he makes via the reveries of his main hero—that credit default swaps were "fil-tered through" collateralized debt obligations (CDOS) and were thus instrumental in the *replication* of bonds backed by home loans. As his hero-narrator says, "There weren't enough Americans with shitty credit taking out loans to satisfy investors' appetite *for the end prod-uct*" (2010, 143, my emphasis). A general point made in Lewis's book is unfortunately overwhelmed by his narrative desire to tell a story of corruption and greed. He shows that investors on opposite ends of the credit default swap market (investors purchasing credit default swaps, often through CDOS, on the one hand, and investors placing bets against the subprime mortgage market, on the other hand) both expected the market to function in the same manner (see 2010, 143–44). That is, there was overall agreement among all market actors on the manner in which value was being produced.

The CDO is an acronym that seems to reference an exceedingly complex and incomprehensible financial tool—an alchemical formula for the production of fictitious value. However, as Annelise Riles reminds us in her clarification of the legal technique that we call collateral, it is best apprehended in terms of the body of doctrines and specialized sets of property rights by which it is constituted and regulated (2011, 49). In her recent, instructive book on "collateral knowledge," Riles visits industry experts (lawyers, bankers, government officials) and studies the forms of documentation (contracts, agreements) that engender the knowledge base and material practice of "collateral," which is essentially devised to "place limits" on the "indeterminacies" of relationships (21). Collateralized debt obligations are structured asset-backed securities; they are bonds issued by legal entities that entail portfolios of other bonds, such as consumer loans for consumer goods, mortgages, and of course student loans. The latter constitute the underlying assets, which serve as collateral in the case of default. Mezzanine CDOs include CDO tranches[13] (consisting of mostly BBB rated subprime mortgage bonds) and synthetic CDOs (consisting of credit default swaps on triple-B rated subprime mortgage bonds). Both were central to the bets placed "against the market," or on the risk of nonpayment. Demand was for the most risk.

How did demand for risk arise? We have insights from those who have inquired into how the demand for risk emerged in the realm of finance, particularly in the late twentieth century. Bill Maurer (1999), for example, has illustrated how, at the end of the last century, a significant shift in practices of securitization occurred: securities clearance and settlement in terms of property rights and negotiability was displaced by risk profiling and practices of insurance (366).[14] Through jurisprudence and economic regulation, the subject of property was redefined "not as the bearer of rights but as a risk profile subject to the disciplinary practice of insurance," giving rise to forms of convertibility and capital mobility, and hence new techniques of securitization. Elaborating on the technical infrastructure, or distributed financial systems, inherent to these practices, Martha Poon (2012) demonstrates how credit default becomes both intelligible and manipulable when certain organizational practices developed by operations researchers are applied to the business of financing consumers and become stable. Standardized forms, such as commercial credit scores (Poon 2012) or contracts that define collateral obligations (Riles 2011), serve as technical infrastructure for novel credit transactions.[15] For instance, layers of standardization establish the conditions under which derivative products known as "swaps" can be developed in relation to complex securities constructed out of consumer loans. Moreover, as Yves Smith notes, "the creation of a standardized credit default swap on mortgages made it feasible to take large subprime short positions," which engendered profits, which incited the creation of more "subprime," which made bets on the risk of nonpayment more profitable (Smith blog post, March 25, 2010).[16] Therefore, even though shorting the market has been denounced with much moral outrage in recent years, many of those bets have inspired much awe, and even a good dose of admiration (cf. Zuckerman 2009). Positions were taken in the swaps market by those now known as "the contrarians," the outsider-heros of Lewis's story, as well as by hedge fund manager John Paulson, who created $15 billion of wealth for his Wall Street firm through what is now touted as "the greatest trade ever." Here we see that the market did not fail and financial instruments were not defective or erroneous. A huge amount of cash was made.[17] What is significant is that raising capital through debt, as opposed to stock issuance, takes on particular forms: the rise of leveraged buyouts in the 1980s took place through funds raised by issuing junk bonds, which began even before the repeal of the Glass-Steagall Act in the 1990s. Poon and Wosnitzer (2012) refer to these practices of producing value through debt during this two-decade span as "the high-leverage movement," where leverage is "a mechanism of linking debt to value" (253) and not an "error perpetuated by elite bankers" or a result of corrupt "Wall Street culture."[18]

But where are houses, or housing assets, in these stories of trades, bets, swaps, and debts? They are *practically* irrelevant to these practices of producing value. In other words, to say that the financial value created was "virtual," or completely divorced from "real value"— houses—is to disregard how houses were practically irrelevant to processes of valuation and the creation of particular forms of wealth, which implies that it is meaningless to try to trace that wealth back to home values, as some kind of "fundamental" value that could be located or determined outside of this system of financial valuation and production.[19] In other words, discerning true value in the materiality of the universe (houses, labor), as an a priori, is distinct from discerning the ways in which forms of value are produced by material systems and technologies, as the burgeoning literature in economic sociology and the social studies of finance shows us.[20]

As argued herein, inspired by Martha Poon's research on how value is constituted through operating systems in consumer credit (2012), houses were not "visible" to these systems. This line of reasoning is implied by Michael Lewis (2010, 98): "The big Wall Street firms— Bear Stearns, Lehman Brothers, Goldman Sachs, Citigroup, and others—had the same goal as any manufacturing business: pay as little as possible for raw material (home loans) and charge as much as possible for their end product (mortgage bonds). The price of the end product was driven by the ratings assigned to it by the models used by Moody's and S&P," which, he notes (99), "didn't actually evaluate the individual home loans, or so much as look at them." The commodities involved were home loans and mortgage bonds. What the financial analysts and their models visualized and assessed were the general characteristics of these loan pools. Brick and mortar were not visible to the financial system that was engaged in valuation.[21]

This modeling or methodology was not an error in the system, nor was it a deviation from the system's underlying principles. This mode of assessment allowed for certain valuations to be produced and it generated possibilities for the production of wealth: it allowed for both risk-based pricing and for gaming or shorting that same system.[22] Lewis's hero is quoted as saying, "When we shorted the bonds, all we had was the pool-level data," to which Lewis adds (2010, 170): "The pool-level data gave you the general characteristics—the average FICO scores, the average loan-to-value ratios, the average numbers of no-doc loans, and so forth—but no view of the individual loans. The pool-level data told you, for example, that 25 percent of the home loans in some pool were insured, but not which loans—the ones likely to go bad or the ones less likely to go. It was impossible to determine how badly the Wall Street firms had gamed the system." Wall Street was working hard to bet against a market that it was working hard to create. And it was generating colossal amounts of wealth in the process: between $200 and $400 billion in subprime-backed CDOS between 2005 and mid-2007, according to Lewis (234).[23] As he then concludes (262), almost in spite of the very moral of his story, "The problem wasn't that Lehman Brothers had been allowed to fail. The problem was that Lehman Brothers had been allowed to succeed."

We are left with a story peopled with "bubblistas" (Clover 2011): those invested in bubbles, which they saw to be bubbles, and those who claim that we could never have perceived the bubble but we nonetheless should have known better—most of whom appear to be one and the same.[24] *"Had anyone known, of course we would have done things differently,"* insists the sardonic Joshua Clover in his tongue-in-cheek ode to the end of empire (2011, emphasis in original). He proffers the typical story of effective knowledge versus a story of failed knowledge: "We know" versus "Had we known." To say, for example, and as I have just argued, that houses were practically irrelevant to the production of fungible debt is not to say that risk products have led us astray from "true" value (homes). The *practical* irrelevance of houses merely implies that housing prices were irrelevant to the pragmatic analytics of valuation, such as the pricing of subprime risk and its associated trades, which suggests that it is meaningless to trace the wealth/debt generated by that system back to home values in an effort to establish some sort of "fundamental" value that could be located or determined outside of this very system of valuation—a material ground from which we have strayed.

Moreover, to say that houses are practically irrelevant is to say that "crisis" is less a claim about error in valuation than a judgment about value, or debt/asset valuation. In this sense, it is a political claim that brought taxpayers into the fray as buyers of last resort, or as the financiers of the dealer banks, desperate to raise capital to make payment on the multilevel trade in synthetic CDOs and hence selling collateral. When banks decided to sell collateral, they created, by definition, a declining market (see Cooper 2008, 100), which is a distinct narrative line from, "When housing prices plummeted, banks started foreclosing on homeowners." Taxpayers' homes were foreclosed upon even though no one can demonstrate that any particular home was tied to any particular CDO or its related forms of trade. Indignation over the fact that taxpayers financed the massive translation of private debt into public debt, via a massive devaluation or expropriation of wealth, lost its political force by replicating the crisis judgment and embarking without hesitation or modesty on the relentless search for deviance from the sure ground of true value and the straight path of uncorrupted history.

FINANCE

Accession to "crisis," which serves to establish a mode of narration, implies that the question of whose house is involved in which forms of debt, and commerce in that debt, has been foreclosed. If we cannot demonstrate these concrete linkages, what justifies the devaluation or foreclosure of certain homes? Some might contend that this question is not raised precisely because we have been colonized by finance itself: financial transactions dominate our lives, we evaluate everyday situations in terms of risk and return, and finance has become both a site of discipline and the means by which we hope to resolve life contingencies (Martin 2002; Martin, Rafferty, and Bryan 2008).[25] This financialization of life is yet another source of disenchantment: the hypothetically autonomous realms of "the social" and of "culture" must be freed from the hegemony of economy.[26] The contemporary crisis is therefore posited as "a crisis of neoliberalism," a shorthand that gloms together "crises of post-Fordism[,] post-national globalization and post-welfarist government" (Clarke 2010, 384).[27] When taken in this way—as a hodgepodge of laissez-faire ideology, free market reform, deregulation, free trade regimes, monetarism, marketization, and so forth—neoliberalism is seen as the purveyor of economism and economic discourse to the detriment of social agencies and cultural movements.[28]

It is hard to fathom how the economic could be anything but social, emerging through associations and translations; it is equally difficult to imagine how one could locate "the social" as a distinct domain; and hence the mere notion of the economy being "disembedded" from "the social" makes no sense (Callon and Latour 1981; Latour 1996, 2005; Latour and Lépinay 2009). That aside, the crude idea of a generalized and always effective neoliberalism occults the ways in which state agencies and infrastructures are crucial to the establishment of markets and economic practice. Moreover, this view equally ignores the ways in which state agencies and infrastructures are essential to processes of financialization, rendering a particular kind of service (finance) as a source of revenue increasingly significant for both financial and nonfinancial firms (Krippner 2011).[29] Private markets and financial activities are coordinated in part through state institutions, the most obvious being contract law, as well as private regulatory solutions, such as international arbitrage, which are now recognized as a discrete form of global financial governance (Riles 2011). And, while unregulated economic activities circumvent forms of state taxation, state-run or public institutions are often generative of unregulated economic activities (Roitman 2005; Palan 2006). In effect, the emergence of subprime mortgage finance has depended greatly on the initiatives of the United States government and state infrastructures (Carruthers and Stinchcombe 1999; Poon 2009). Instead of assuming that the subprime mortgage market was a purely free market affair, Martha Poon shows how "what might look like the spontaneous rise of a 'free' capital market divested of direct government intervention, has been thoroughly embedded in the concerted movement of technological apparatuses" that originated with government-sponsored enterprises. As she says, "It was on the authority of the institutions' guidelines, their initiatives in interface design, as well as their dirty, hands-on involvement as a driver of RMBS [residential mortgage-backed securities] production that the market was made" (2009, 669 and 666; and see Acharya et al. 2011).

In her study of financialization, Greta Krippner (2011) counters the notion that deregulation led to economic crisis, offering a reversal in interpretation: through an exceptionally thorough review of the elaboration of various policy regimes, she shows how particular situations, such as domestic distributional conflict or political problems of credit allocation, led to deregulation so as to incite credit expansion.[30] In this somewhat familiar story (cf. Arrighi, Harvey), deregulation is taken to be the means to ensure the extension of credit, or recapitalization. Though, unlike Arrighi and Harvey, Krippner does not tag these instances as cycles of capitalism; she is primarily concerned with the acts and decisions produced by policy regimes. Krippner documents how the turn to finance was not a voluntaristic move on the part of a seamless state; efforts to solve problems of capital availability and capital allocation were constantly renewed through the construction of various policy regimes, most often entailing disaccord and resulting in the elaboration of unanticipated forms of regulation and market devices. Here, finance is not portrayed as a virtual world of fictive capital. Krippner specifies (4) that, in her account, the term "financial" "references the provision (or transfer) of capital in expectation of future interests, dividends, or capital gains." And "productive" refers to "the range of activities involved in the production or trade of commodities." In this sense, financial activities are not necessarily delinked or separate from the realm of production: much (though not absolutely all) financial activity takes place to support production; and the realms of financial and productive activity are co-constituted. Even though we might be able to distinguish between a loan on a car and the revenues generated from the sale of the car, she remarks, one facilitates the other. "To suggest that the economy has become financialized is to claim that the balance between these two sets of activities has swung strongly toward finance, not that the financial economy has become entirely uncoupled from production" (4).

Those who claim to witness the thoroughgoing financialization of our lives tend to discount the co-constitution of discursive and material formations. They discern a radical disjuncture between "economic nomenclature" and "the real economy" (Hayward 2010, 284).[31]

Most recently, this distinction between appearance and reality has been correlated with financial models (value at risk models, derivatives), on the one hand, and real value, which is often harder to locate, on the other. Liquidity or not, crisis is taken to be a problem of true value. From a cultural studies perspective, crisis denotes the reduction of life forms to pure economic value; we must save social and cultural value from economic reductionism so as to redeem life. In an essay entitled "Modernity and Commensuration," published recently in a widely circulated special issue of *Cultural Studies*, Lawrence Grossberg (2010, 296–97) writes that what he calls a "conjuncturalist" understanding of contemporary crisis helps us to understand both the context as well as the "articulations" that constitute that very context. He thus aims to apprehend crisis *in* history (context) and crisis *of* history (articulations that constitute context). For Grossberg, crisis must be apprehended as "an event" both at the level of history and as "an event" at the level of the constitution of that history—as conjunctural and as epistemological.

Arguing for an analysis that would account for both the occurrence of the "housing bubble" as well as the conditions of possibility for the occurrence of the housing bubble, Grossberg (2010, 299) apprehends crisis on the level of liquidity and on the level of epistemology:

> The common assumption is that the crisis begins with the collapse of the housing bubble—as if there were not signs of a crisis in corporate and global capitalism before that—and the realization that no one seemed to know the value of many of the financial instruments that banks had created to leverage and securitize their mortgage (and as we are constantly hearing whispered in the background, credit card and corporate) debt. This was assumed to be and was experienced as a breakdown of the relations of credit to collateral. But I want to argue later that this liquidity crisis, when placed at the feet of the instruments themselves, as it were, might be better seen as the result of a failed solution to a real conjunctural problem: the problem of the calculation of value.

Not concerned with the actual production of particular forms of value through pragmatic analytics, Grossberg discerns a crisis of valuation, which he defines as a crisis of commensuration most easily surmised in the realm of the derivative. This now common opinion that the derivative, which is amplified to an encompassing "derivative logic," has wrought havoc on our stable world is understood in terms of processes of commensuration. Following other prominent scholars, Grossberg take derivatives to be "a new incarnation of the commodity form" (see Pryke and Allen 2000; LiPuma and Lee 2004; Martin 2007; and especially Bryan and Rafferty 2006, 2007). Consequently, he defines derivatives as computational devices for processes of capital commensuration (i.e., between different forms of assets to establish pricing relationships), which, through a "non-dialectical logic of calculation," give rise to "the expansion of a universe of values put into relations of adequation or commensuration" (2010, 305).[32] This potentially infinite system poses the problem of a universal standard, which Grossberg explains as follows: "The key to my argument is that the contemporary explosion and use of derivatives is at least in part a response to, first, the move from gold to money as the universal equivalent on a global scale and second, the denial of the universal equivalent. On this argument, the current credit crisis can be seen, perhaps, as the failure of the derivative, which itself must be located within a larger configuration of the contemporary impossibility of a universal commensuration" (315).

The derivative is the subject of a particular, conjunctural crisis as well as a metaphor for a crisis in the constitution of historical possibility. In Grossberg's terms: "the derivative and its crisis can be seen as an articulation of, as articulated to at least two vectors of change that are constituting the contemporary conjuncture as a problem-space(s), defined by the struggle over/for an other modernity" (314). In other words, this is a struggle in history (for stable value, for truth value) and it is a struggle of history (for the future, for empirical grounds). Grossberg (2007, 2010) refers to this as a struggle over temporality itself, vexed by the means to establish a stable, reliable relationship between the present and the future. Moreover, this conjucture is equally said to be a struggle over so-called multiple modernities; the proliferation of values; the dislocation of labor value over other, less material sources of value; and contention over concepts and practices of value (2010, 318).[33] Although, for Grossberg, derivative logic should not be seen as mystifying, he nonetheless takes caution when it comes to the appearances produced by the derivative, on the one hand, and hard reality, on the other. He therefore concludes that the contemporary crisis is a crisis of modernity, or a contest between multiple modernities, because there is no real, material value—no houses with intrinsic value, no home for value—because there is no universal equivalent.

Other studies of subprime mortgage lending have endeavored to skirt this presumed fundamental difference between real and virtual value forms. Paul Langley, who has published considerable work on global financial markets and the emergence of particular forms of consumer credit in the United States and the United Kingdom, for example, takes a slightly different approach from Grossberg: rather than decry the dislocation of value, he seeks to understand the production of value through financial instruments for risk-based pricing. He asks (2008, 470), somewhat echoing my query above, "if the boom in sub-prime lending can appear as so deleterious and deadly in the context of the current crisis, how did it materialize over more than a decade as a largely undisputed and extremely profitable venture?" He replies by reviewing risk-based pricing practices, securitization, and originate-to-distribute-models, before turning to "the interest-only and adjustable rate mortgage products which came to predominate in sub-prime lending," and which gave rise to mortgagors who, "as leveraged investors, responsibly and entrepreneurially embraced risk in a rising property market" (472). Langley is not concerned to denounce the financialization of human life so as to reclaim a culture untarnished by economism or social relations purified of economic calculations. He is interested in the co-constitution of discursive and material formations; he thus seeks to understand "how the historically specific agency of sub-prime lending came to be assembled," and inquires into the socio-technical assemblage, or the heterogeneous objects and agencies (models, markets, consumers, concepts) that made subprime lending "appear as a legitimate part of the contemporary financial markets" (472).[34]

In view of this aim to account for both the effective production of certain practices and their efficacy in the world, the verb "appear" ("appear as legitimate") is disconcerting. Langley claims to show that interest-only adjustable rate mortgages (ARMS), which have initial "teaser" interest rates that adjust (or are reset) to a higher rate for the remainder of the mortgage term, emerged as "products that enabled the inclusion of borrowers as agents within the mortgage and housing markets" (479). To quote his reasoning at length:

> Indeed, underpinning affordability products in general and interest-only ARMS in particular is the assumption that house prices will rise, creating equity for the owner-occupier who can "cash out" this equity in order to meet future and rising repayments. Reducing repayments in the short term is thus not simply a responsible affordability strategy, but also an entrepreneurial strategy of leveraged investment that *embraces the risk* of house price changes. At the same time, the entrepreneurial manipulation of outstanding obligations is an important self-discipline within an interest-only ARM, as the mortgagor will take up a "refi" before the reset date when monthly payments rise. House price rises during the initial option period are assumed to have created equity that can be "cashed out" to meet the future and higher repayments of a refinanced mortgage." (479, my emphasis)

From this description, we can conclude that financial tools (ARMS) and a particular market (subprime mortgage) worked precisely as they should have—that is, as they were designed to work. In other words, this market and its constitutive practices did not appear to be legitimate; this market and its constitutive practices were legitimate.

Langley notes that many financial journalists and policy makers focused on the failure of inference as the cause of the collapse of the U.S. subprime market; these commentators argued that financial analysts lacked sufficient "historical data" necessary for inferences to calculate future probabilities of default for various categories of risk. As Langley points out, this view assumes that future uncertainties could be priced through a perfected practice of inference, or, as I would put it, that true prices could be known outside of pricing practices. His view is that this misguided interpretation overlooks the contradictions that lie at the very heart of risk-based pricing and interest-only adjustable rate mortgages. From this point of view, crisis is not located in the failure of knowledge; it resides in the models themselves: "Contradictions of calculative devices of risk" (risk-based pricing and ARMs) exposed borrowers to extreme uncertainties (interest rates, house prices). Langley's point is not merely that securitization generated an untenable number of poorly screened or mispriced individual loans. Rather, his point is that "even the effective screening and securitization of default risks was itself contradictory, and the incapacity of the risk calculations of the capital markets to address collective future uncertainties was always present" (484). One might surmise that "contradictions" refers to the disjuncture between case-by-case risk analysis and securitization, on the one hand, and the analysis of collective future uncertainties, on the other. But this is not clear. At any rate, contradictions, in this account, produce crisis; they are not quite the motor of history, as in Marxist-inspired analyses, but the term signifies a discrepancy between what is and what should or could be. Therefore, while Langley sets out to demonstrate the effective production of value, in both its economic and anthropological senses, he embarks on a sociology of error: "Each set of [risk] devices is shown to have been unable to capture future uncertainties through apparently rational and scientific calculations of risk. Risk-based pricing failed, in its own terms, to price default risk effectively" (473). But if we face a "necessarily uncertain future" (481), then in what sense could these devices fail? And if we take the practice of risk-based pricing on its own terms, in what sense could it misprice? But more important, as Martha Poon affirms with regard to uncertain futures, "We do not face financial risk, we make financial risk within controlled environments."[35] Langley's "alternative critical reading of the crisis," while informative, is perhaps not all that alternative in its quest for antimonies. His disquiet about the alleged contradictions that surface due to the inability to "capture the uncertain future" rejoins Lawrence Grossberg's foreboding about competing value forms—both are concerned to explain crisis as a problem of competing or incommensurate worlds.

Throughout these narratives of struggle and proliferating values, of uncertain futures and contradictions, crisis is never itself challenged. Crisis is the motor of history; it is the means to signify change. It is the blind spot from which to apprehend history—the place of a distinction. As Koselleck would have it, and as is reiterated in the introductory essay to the special issue of *Cultural Studies*, which published Grossberg's searching essay, crisis offers "the promise of history" (Hayward 2010, 284). That is, as John Clarke notes in the same volume (2010, 383), crisis is not an "innocent" term: it invites us "to perceive particular phenomena, causes, tendencies and potential routes to salvation." Crisis has a sort of sanctified power. It is set forth with unquestioned faith as the means to define, locate, and observe historical change; and it unquestionably signifies that change itself. The conjunctural analysis pursued by Lawrence Grossberg and the cultural economy analysis pursued by Paul Langley are a means to describe change in terms of articulations and contradictions, which do not necessarily adhere to a dialectical logic. Instead, multiple logics give rise to a unified conjuncture that is provisional and heterogeneous. Grossberg therefore describes the contemporary conjuncture as being "in crisis" because of the failure of unicity, no matter its temporary (historical) character. And he describes the contemporary conjuncture as a crisis "of" history itself because of the failure of knowledge of the present—it is a crisis of epistemology. Langley describes the contemporary conjuncture as being "in crisis" because of the failure of prediction, which also can be understood as a failure of knowledge, or the ability to know an uncertain future—what he calls "the discrepency between promise and outcome" (489).[36] One can only conclude, as does Grossberg (2010, 310): "To mis-analyze a conjuncture, to misidentify its problem-space is to fail to understand what's going on and likely, to fail to formulate political strategies that can get us from here to some other imagined/better place." Crisis serves a philosophy of history.

Finance, financialization, derivatives, and even inept calculative devices are said to have brought our ways of knowing into crisis, which is denoted as the impossibility of commensuration. We are said to be facing "the challenge of ontological pluralism" (Grossberg 2010, 323). Is this not an everyday challenge? Is ontological pluralism resolved in our effective practices, in the pragmatics of creating common worlds, through recourse to universal equivalents or a universal standard? Are there ways of apprehending our pragmatics of valuation in terms other than an impasse of ontological pluralism and the logics of crisis? This is not a new question.[37] But impulsive and instinctive recourse to crisis belies the disavowal of noncontingent grounds for judgment. As I sought to make clear above, with reference to Koselleck's conceptual history of crisis, the temporalization of history, or temporal understanding of the relationship between knowledge and action, or theory and practice—the claim that we can act "on" history to transform it—remains contingent upon the concept of crisis. We persevere in the hope that we can perceive the moments when history is alienated in terms of its philosophy—that is, that we can perceive a dissonance between historical events and representations of those events. "Finance capital is unmoored from reality" (Martin 2010a, 427), but the grounds for the knowledge of unmooring are never quite substantiated. What constitutes *proof of knowledge* of this unmooring of reality? And the ways that finance or, to be more specific, financial models and practices serve to generate and stabilize particular objects of knowledge is generally not considered at all. We are left in a chasm: perplexed and immobilized by the supposed radical dissonance between the value of houses and the value of derivatives of houses.

SUBJECTS

Apparently capable of observing the abyss, some observers insist that what is at stake at present for homeowners and taxpayers is either the experience of crisis or the crisis of subjectivity. These commentators urge us not to lose sight of the fact that the events of 2007–9 brought about a "subjective crisis" (Hardt and Negri 2009), a crisis of the neoliberal subject (Clarke 2009), or a crisis of a form of liberal modern subjectivity (Grossberg 2010). In keeping with the conviction that crisis denotes a situation in which the contingency of truth claims is revealed, or the grounds for truth claims are made bare and the limits of intelligibility are potentially subverted or transgressed, the epistemological crisis is manifest in the crisis of finance. According to these interpretations, the expropriated homeowner is a subject in crisis, with no stable grounds of truth value, staring into the abyss of the limits of intelligibility.

Here again, crisis is the unexamined point of departure for narration. It is a blind spot for the production of knowledge about what constitutes historical significance and about what constitutes social or historical meaning. This manner of taking crisis to be a state of affairs, or an enduring condition, implies that crisis is not an event that occurs in a given context, but that it is itself an experience of historical time. In other words, crisis is itself a context, such that we are "the subjects of times of crisis" (Mbembe and Roitman 1995; and see Greenhouse, Mertz, and Warren 2002; Lomnitz 2003; Vigh 2008; Khan 2009). Posited in this way, crisis is the point from which hermeneutics or anthropology begins: crisis is the means to access both "the social" and "experience" because it entails the disclosure of the constitutive conditions of human practice.[38] The anthropologist Henrik Vigh makes this plea that crisis be the basis for hermeneutic or anthropological knowledge in a programmatic statement, entitled "Crisis and Chronicity." Here, Vigh proposes a move from "placing a given instance of crisis in context" to "seeing crisis as a context," by which he means "a terrain of action and meaning rather than an aberration" (2008, 8). This move implies that crisis becomes a norm: crisis is an ongoing experience or an enduring condition—a postulate that is not unlike the conclusion that the normativity of capitalism is permanent crisis.[39] However, as Vigh himself notes, the very notion of constant crisis implodes the concept of crisis. Because crisis no longer signifies critical, historical change (a turning point), one ends in an oxymoronic "ordered disorder." Vigh welcomes this implosion of the concept (while nevertheless retaining the term) as a means of "freeing the concept from its temporal confines" (2008, 9). To unleash the concept of crisis from time would clearly be an unprecedented form of freedom, but the claim seems to entirely disregard the conceptual history of the term, or Reinhart Koselleck's point that crisis is necessarily a temporal concept.

The programmatic statement recently taken up by Vigh is common, if not foundational, to social science practice. That position purports that crisis is a point of departure for both anthropological insights, produced by social scientists, on the one hand, as well as a point of departure for the production of rules, norms, and meaning generated by local people themselves, or by those being observed, on the other.[40] This approach is in keeping with the long-standing tradition of social science theory, for which crisis serves as a mediation between theory and practice (cf., for example, Benhabib 1986). As was indicated above, because crisis is taken to be an instance when the contingency of truth claims are made bare, it presumably grants access to a social world: "When crisis becomes context the order of our social world becomes in other words questioned and substituted by multiple contestations and interpretations leading to the recognition that our world is in fact plural rather than singular: social rather than natural" (Vigh 2008, 16). This claim reiterates the approach to critique associated with contemporary critical theory, pragmatic sociology, or post-structuralism, all of which take reflexivity to be crucial to practices of justification and the formation of critique. But self-reflexivity is inherent to praxis; it is not necessarily or inevitably contingent upon crisis.

If we accept that self-reflexivity is inherent to praxis, we can then ask a series of questions: do homeowners have a reflexive relationship to "credit" or to "liquidity" or to "collateral" or to "volatility"? And has this reflexivity brought about a breach or rupture in the *forms of knowledge and material technologies* that ground their economic lives and financial practice? These are genuine questions; we don't have answers to them. And therefore it is not clear how we can assert that there is a "crisis of subjectivity," engendered by the alleged virtual world of finance or the supposed dislocation of value brought on by financial practices, until we can describe displacements or ruptures in knowledge formation or manners of producing valid statements. It seems premature, then, to narrate the crisis of the neoliberal subject. Even though home foreclosure self-help groups did spring up across America, it is doubtful that these gatherings served as anything but strategies for transferring personal funds to private banks so as to reestablish one's personal "liquidity."[41] Activist organizations, such as Americans for Fairness in Lending or the National Association of Consumer Advocates, have taken issue with the privileging of investors' interests over debtors and homeowners, insisting that securitization contracts impair forbearance, or the delay of foreclosure. Commenting on this dilemma, Paul Langley (2008, 490) concludes: "There is little scope for co-responsibility between lender and borrower at moments of distress, and the long-standing legal principle that the borrower is primarily responsible for meeting outstanding obligations is enshrined in new ways."[42] Precisely, the claim to crisis and accession to that claim serves to enshrine long-standing principles, sometimes in new ways: in this instance, it serves to justify forbearance (delay of foreclosure) and precludes the *outright refutation of the very idea of foreclosure* as a relevant or legitimate concept and action.

Of course some taxpayers took to the streets to contest the public bailout of private banks, most notably, at least initially, in European capitals. These protests, though sometimes widespread, did not amount to a social movement articulating an alternative crisis narrative. In 2011, the Occupy Wall Street movement emerged and spread through American cities. The "We Are the 99%" slogan was an effective mobilizing claim, which made visible a sense of majority opinion and a claim to rectify drastic and increasing economic and social inequalities.[43] Regrettably, widespread dissent did not give rise to an effective, divergent interpretation of the *significance* of the crisis, much less discordant manners of apprehending its constitutive terms: volatility, risk, liquidity, asset bubble, credit crunch, foreclosure, default, and, for my European friends, austerity. We cannot apprehend epistemological crisis because there has been no fundamental transformation in forms of knowledge production: there has been no transformation, for instance, of the way in which "credit risk" is produced for people as a practicable, actionable category in their lives. As far as we know, there has been no *transformation in the intelligibility* of "liquidity" or "volatility," much less "default."

The salient point is not to deny the lived trauma of those who lost homes and jobs. *To the contrary, the point is to take note of the effects of the claim to crisis, and to take note of the effects of our very accession to that judgment.* The forms of critique engendered by crisis serve to politicize interest groups for a critique of capitalism. This is a politics of crisis. Moving beyond this politics of crisis, one might insist that effective forms of critique would instead engender new forms of knowledge such that, for instance, the very boundary between "the economic" and "the political" would be reorganized or transformed. But this has not obtained. The crisis of the subject—be it neoliberal or indebted capitalist—entails an epistemological crisis that could only be apprehended through cognizance of a transformation in the rules for making meaningful statements (Foucault 1972, 1973). If crisis obtains, the very question posed by the Occupy Wall Street movement and by groups or individuals mobilized in other countries—which social actors should bear the burden of a fading prosperity?—would no longer have significance for the narration of history.

Contemporary claims to a crisis in prevailing forms of knowledge take issue with the adequacy of particular modes of organization and practice. As we have seen, they are post hoc denunciations. Not being demonstrations that the production and organization of knowledge itself have undergone transformation, or that prevailing manners of producing valid statements ("this is risk," "this is volatility," "this is default") have been transformed, these narratives posit crisis as an a priori. Crisis is taken to be the basis for a method, permitting and justifying narration in terms of analogous historical events and logical recurrence.[44] To return, again, to Koselleck's conceptual history, once crisis achieves status as a freestanding historico-philosophical concept, it is practiced as the referent from which history is both apprehended and comprehended. In other words, if history is constituted out of its own conditions of knowledge and action, or out of the criterion of time, this history in-and-for-itself nonetheless requires a referent from which movement and transformation, or historical change itself, can be posited. In this predicament of signifying human history, crisis serves as a transcendental placeholder; it is the a priori that both marks historical events and qualifies history as such. Thus while the historian is the judge of what constitutes an event, history is posited as the ultimate form of judgment—a judgment we take to be effected retrospectively through error and deviation, or in terms of the alienation of humanity from history. But, as I asked above: what is the burden of proof for such judgments? Not only is the judgment of "crisis" as historical transformation necessarily a post hoc affair, but also the grounds for knowledge of crisis are neither elucidated nor questioned. For the accounts reviewed herein, crisis is posited as an a priori; and thus, ultimately, contemporary narratives of crisis elude the question of *how one can know crisis in history* as well as the question of *how one can know crisis itself.* That is, crisis raises the dilemma of the very possibility of bearing witness, or of representation.

The dilemma of this impossibility of bearing witness to crisis is not novel—it is often shorthanded as the "unsayability" of Auschwitz. But it is an unexamined problem for contemporary narrative accounts. Also unexamined, though, are the ways in which witnessing is purported to redeem meaning (of events, of suffering) for history.[45] These claims to bearing witness and to crisis assume that crisis has a status in history and that crisis is accessible as an object of knowledge.[46] In that sense, crisis is not taken to be an aporia, or the very *impossibility of representation*—such as the inability to utter, to speak, to narrate, to write. Instead, crisis is posited as a non-locus from which *to signify* contingency and as a *self-authorizing ground* for accounts of the emergent. This presupposition is highly reminiscent of what Dominick LaCapra (2004, 176) discerns in Giorgio Agamben's writing on the problem of bearing witness: "In Agamben one often has the sense that he begins with the presupposition of the aporia or paradox, which itself may at times lose its force and its insistence in that it does not come about through the breakdown or experienced impasse in speaking, writing, or trying to communicate but instead seems to be postulated at the outset. In other words, a prepackaged form seems to seek its somewhat arbitrary content. And the paradox and the aporia become predictable components of a fixated methodology." The presupposition of a form—a paradox, an aporia, crisis—establishes the slate upon which the act of witnessing potentially can occur.[47] As a logical category, crisis serves method. And not being elaborated as a philosophical category, crisis is a narrative category.[48] As an a priori, crisis is the place from which to posit a future.

CHAPTER 3

CRISIS

Refrain!

NONCRISIS NARRATION

What are the possibilities generated by suspending crisis as the foundation of narration and critique? Without pretense to an answer to that far-reaching question, I conclude this book by exploring narratives that do not have recourse to a sociology of error and post hoc denunciation—those that do not discern historical significance in terms of human error and ethical failure. To do so, and with limited recourse to such formulations, I turn to recent analyses that posit risk as the basis of crisis in our world today. This position is widespread in both social science and popular accounts of contemporary history: risk is the permanent peril.[1]

Systemic risk has a long history in the banking sector. In a précis on systemic risk in consumer finance, Martha Poon (2010)[2] points out that "in finance, systemic risk has traditionally referred to the possibility that a loss incurred at one banking institution could propagate outwards, unleashing a chain of events through which the financial system as a whole would fail. Systemic risk should not be conflated with an economic downturn or dramatic losses, which are natural parts of what is at stake in financial activity. Rather it is concerned with the catastrophic loss of functioning in the system of finance itself, thought to be triggered by an event occurring within a single firm. (The classic case in this model is a bank run.)." She further notes that the emergence of integrated global capital markets has transformed the notion of systemic risk, drawing an array of actors from both within and outside the banking industry into the systemic arena. Her key distinction is between the realm of banking institutions that could be characterized by a hermetic world called "finance" and the current realm of finance constituted by global socio-technological assemblages.[3]

Systemic risk is now cited as a primordial agent of history in contemporary crisis accounts; and it is increasingly denoted as "volatility." What is at stake in this denotation is the risk carried by a class of assets and/or liabilities, or by a portfolio thereof, as well as the risk carried by liquidity prices. The measure of risk is a variable that indicates price volatility of underlying asset returns *over time*; it likewise can serve to measure price volatility of liquidity *over time*. In that sense, it is a measure of how quickly specific encoded, or predetermined, values change: projections of change *over time*. According to this view, crisis is equated with the mispricing of risk (cf. Greenspan 2007, 507; Shiller 2008) or with the failure to properly value liquidity in time (Scholes 2009). In 2007–9, it was said, with much fascination and wonder, that there was literally "no market" due to the inability of analysts and models to evaluate relations of credit and collateral—that is, the inability to calculate value. Likewise, the freeze-up of interbank short-term lending was depicted as a similar lack of a market. Crisis obtains through *error*: it is either mis-valuation or it is the failure to determine value.

In a general sense, financial instability, and thus the "crisis of 2007–9," is taken to be inherent to the mechanics of the asset and debt markets. Self-reinforcing asset-debt cycles are described as the spirit of the banking system.[4] For neo-Keynesians, systemic risk, which should be managed by a central bank, is envisaged in terms similar to those employed by neo-Marxists: "If the self-reinforcing credit cycles described here exist, this policy of endless credit expansion becomes dangerously destabilizing. As each successive attempted credit contraction is successfully counteracted with engineered stimulus, the economy is pushed into a state of ever greater indebtedness, presenting the risk of a still more violent contraction in the future. Over time, a policy of always maximizing economic activity implies a constantly increasing debt stock and progressively more fragile financial system" (Cooper 2008, 122). By this account, systemic risk inheres in the instability of constant credit creation, which is essential to an expanding economy. For neo-Marxists, systemic risk lies in the underlying contradictions of capital accumulation, which require a means of transcending the limits to capital flows encountered in capitalist expansion, found today in financial innovation and the augmentation of credit by the financial sector (Harvey 2010). In an abbreviated presentation of his recent work, David Harvey (2011, 89) states that "systemic risk," newly discovered by liberal economists, has long been the subject of Marxian analysis, theorized in terms of the fundamental contradictions of capital accumulation. Indeed, for neo-Keynesian analysis, risk underlies the permanent threat of crisis and is represented by the "bust" metaphor of combustion-sounding boom-and-bust cycles; when crises occur, they are due to errors in central bank policy, or a failure to regulate the endless rotations of an economy. While for neo-Marxist analysis, risk is equated with the tendency toward crisis that is endemic to capitalism, being structural and necessary to historical transformation; crisis is due to an erroneous model of compound growth and harbors the missed revolution.

No matter its metaphors or manifestations, risk is necessarily, like crisis, the subject of post hoc denunciation. Probability distributions are said to have been in the wrong place only after "crisis" has been pronounced. Risk distributions are said to have been too narrow only after "crisis" has been pronounced. Asset bubbles are said to have swelled to untenable proportions only after they have burst, when prices plummet and "crisis" is pronounced. The risk posed to capitalist accumulation, or the limits encountered by profitable private investment in its search for future capitalization, is only narrated once compound rates of growth are said to have reached historical inflexion points, always a post hoc reading of a diagram, and always after "crisis" has been pronounced. Perilous risk is inevitably, and not very usefully, signaled after economic decline. Risk, uncertainty, and crisis characterize the world in which we act; our knowledge is inevitably insufficient, inadequate; we thus denounce this failure of rationality, of reason.

Risk is thought to be "out there." If it is not located correctly, measured accurately, or regulated properly, we will not navigate its odds—it will be revealed to us; it is the object of our overcoming.[5] This presupposition of the ontological status of risk is part and parcel of contemporary financial crisis narratives. Risk is assumed; and fervent, if sometimes arcane, debates are pursued as to distinctions between risk and uncertainty, or the extent to which, through probabilistic forms of knowledge, we can make distinctions between calculable forms of indeterminancy (risk) versus non-calculable forms of indeterminancy (uncertainty). This distinction between calculable, or probabilizable, forms of indeterminacy and non-calculable, or non-probabilizable, forms of indeterminacy—or between risk and uncertainty—was put forth by Frank Knight in his famous *Risk, Uncertainty and Profit*, authored in 1921, and leading to the lofty-sounding expression "Knightian uncertainty."[6] Michael Power comments on this assumption that risk is out there, noting the problem with the practice of presupposing the ontological value of Knight's distinction: "The ambition of risk analysis to model recalcitrant or complex interacting hazard phenomena effectively transforms acts of god into possibilities for rational decision-making and policy. From this point of view, Knight's famous distinction between risk and uncertainty, which is often *the starting point for definitional anxieties* about risk, *must be taken as historical and changing* rather than invariant" (2007, 13, my emphasis).[7] In his recent book, *Organized Uncertainty*, Power examines the "abstraction, rationalization, and expansion of risk management ideas" under way since the 1990s so as to illustrate how "organized uncertainty" has come to be designated as "risk." He is interested in the discursive operations through which a particular concept of "risk" comes to signify particular events, which it purportedly describes (Power 2007, 4, following Knights and Vurdubakis 1993). "In this way," Power explains, "the enquiry is directed away from the noun *per se*, and its various semantic bewitchments, towards the role of managerial and administrative *practices* organized for the explicit purpose of representing and handling risk" (2007 and cf. Baker and Simon 2002; Garland 2003). Risk, then, is not taken to be an ontological entity that exists as a "thing" in the world.[8]

In this emphasis on practice, Michael Power disposes of scholastic conversations about risk versus uncertainty, which have become fashionable in recent debates about the elusive origins of the crisis. Power (2007, 5) argues that "the distinction between uncertainty and risk does not refer to two different classes of 'object'. Nor does it quite match Knight's distinction based on the availability, or not, of probabilistic knowledge. The distinction has to do with a dynamic of organizing to produce decidability and actionability." Power contends that risk is *produced* by management systems, which are devised for identification, assessment, and mitigation, making risk an object of standards, measure, audit, and eventually claims about a state of affairs.[9] In contrast to Ulrich Beck and Anthony Giddens, who take risk to be a primary mode of sociopolitical organization in the world today, or what they call "risk society," as noted above, Power argues that "the organization of uncertainty in the form of risk management designs and standards is related to expectations of governance and demands for defendable, auditable process" (2007, 6).[10] Power explains clearly (2007, 4 and 21–22) how his account of the emergence of "designs for risk management" cannot be equated with these arguments for a new "risk society": instead of taking risk as something to be governed via management techniques so as to diminish or avert harm, such management processes produce risk and serve ideals of opportunity, performance, gain, and value. His rejection of the ontology of risk implies that one cannot easily claim that the world is objectively riddled by increased risk today.

An appreciation of how risk is produced and pursued as a form of value is crucial to thinking about possible alternative accounts of contemporary financial practice, as will be clarified below. These accounts need not proceed from an assumption of error; they indicate, instead, the efficacy of certain systems for knowledge production. The question remains: how are risk objects produced as such? How is something designated "risk" produced as a visible, actionable category engendering certain forms of decision making? In Power's nice summation (2007, 22–23, my emphases):

> In both the private and public sectors the concept of risk is being enrolled in a new focus on *outcomes and performance*. In the private sector this is visible in efforts to link investments in control activities to organizational objectives and *value creation* within frameworks for enterprise-wide risk management (ERM). The world of insurance has been similarly transformed over time as part of the *selling of risk management* (Baker and Simon, 2002). In the UK public sector "risk", rather like customer responsiveness, is emerging as the basis for *self-challenging management practices* in the absence of direct competitive pressures. Large consultancy firms sell risk management designs as much more than a preventative technology.[11]

To better understand how risk obtains empirical status—or the production of risk as a practicable entity—it is best to think of financial models, instruments, and methods as devices for formatting and creating contexts, as opposed to assuming that they operate in a given context (Callon and Muniesa 2002; MacKenzie 2006; Callon, Millo, and Muniesa 2007). In other words, financial devices are not used in contexts; they create contexts: the model and its context are co-constituted. By accounting for this process of co-constitution, one can likewise account for the materialization of (often unprecedented) practices (evaluation, standardization), which are manifest in, for example, the production of market segments or financial products, such as risk. These "market devices" (Callon, Millo, and Muniesa 2007) are distributed technical arrangements, emerging from socio-technical assemblages, which participate in the production of calculative spaces and agencies, thus generating and sustaining processes of qualification and valuation. Because quantification requires a priori qualification—or the assessment of qualities that can then be measured, calibrated, standardized, and calculated—market devices are not purely quantitative, as is often supposed.[12] These devices are constituted by socio-technical assemblages comprised of both financial and nonfinancial actors, instruments, and institutions; they are concrete, pragmatic devices (*dispositifs*) and distributed agencies (*agencements*) that do not exist outside of, or prior to, their enactment, or performance, in practice.

In that sense, accounts of market devices are *not demonstrations of the effects of modes of calculation on human practice*, as is implied in the onslaught of denunciatory crisis narratives, which presume that models, equations, and quantitative risk management systems produced error—erroneous value, erroneous assessment, erroneous judgment—and allowed economics, finance, and quantitative value to lead human conduct astray. One might say, instead, that the proverbial bank run is not due to an error of the model, but is rather due to the execution of the model in practice (cf. MacKenzie and Millo 2001; Millo and MacKenzie 2007).[13] And to say that is to pursue an approach in terms of practice that is distinct from interpretations of models—be they risk management models or any sort of financial model—in terms of error.[14] The socio-technical assemblages that work to format and stabilize agreement on evaluative principles and on a quality (e.g., risk as a practicable entity) *is an achievement* that allows for common calculation, or coordinated calculative agencies, to come into being.[15]

Demonstrating the *how* of that achievement is a challenging and labor-intensive project: it entails extensive research that requires specific technical knowledge pertaining to the object of study—technical proficiency that is typically black-boxed by social scientists. But more significantly, as I am striving to make clear herein, the postulate of crisis seems to obviate the need for such technical accounts. In order to bring home that point, in what follows, I turn to an example of one such study, which documents the technical constitution of "subprime," so that we can glimpse the stakes of an account that suspends crisis as the foundation of narration and critique. In the interest of clarity—and, as an aside, because such studies contribute to our financial literacy[16]—I present this illustration at length.

In a meticulous study of a brand of commercial consumer credit analytics known as consumer risk FICO scores, Martha Poon (forthcoming) shows how U.S. consumer credit risk has become transferable as a commodity, or a financial product.[17] She details, in one particular case, how "subprime" risk emerged as a market segment in mortgage finance. She likewise traces the process through which FICO scores were incorporated into automated underwriting systems, eventually becoming industry-wide distributed and collective market devices. A market that is able to assess risk is a market that develops methods for the pricing and trading of risk, rather than merely selecting out for high-quality loans, as defined by government agencies (Fannie Mae and Freddie Mac). Poon's research tracks "the technical constitution of an investment subprime" (2009, 655) and accounts for the recent unprecedented nature of subprime liquidity. Rather than setting out to locate error in the model, erroneous human behavior, or errant historical pathways—"instead of presuming what it is that is collapsing" (655)—she demonstrates how the realization of FICO as a common calculative tool in mortgage valuation entailed the stabilization of a common interpretation of the scores, which clarifies how subprime finance became a network of *investment-grade* lending, or an *effective* means of producing value.

Because "there are as many potential solutions to a problem of valuation as there are participating agents" (656), Poon takes pains to illustrate the concerted work that simultaneously changes the lending context and leads to the selective reduction of calculative multiplicity. As she says (656), "To create liquidity in any circuit of mortgage finance—government sponsored or otherwise—numerous agents must come to similar understandings of the value of the asset backed paper so that it can be successive[ly] transferred between market participants." Emphasizing how risk calculation enables and facilitates the act of financial exchange over the search for errors in calculation, Poon traces the emergence of shared understandings of the qualities of goods between heterogeneous actors, which are assembled via government-sponsored entities, private firms, and market tools, such as specialized underwriting software. In this way, she is able to indicate how traditional, exclusionary practices of credit-control-by-screening were displaced by gradated practices of credit-by-risk. She summarizes this process as follows: "Where subprime lending required overriding the very judgment that was central to control-by-screening (since by definition a subprime loan was a mortgage that has been screened out), in a regime of control-by-risk, subprime lending became an exercise in risk management within a newly created space of calculative possibility. Under control-by-risk, managerial decision making was no longer confined to approving or withholding loans, but was extended to the exploitation of stabilized grades of credit quality accessed through scores to create multiple borrowing options tailored to accommodate varying levels of risk" (656–57). As "creditworthiness" came to be expressed through a gradated risk, the score scale became "a generator of calculative possibility" (667), giving rise to a novel chain of (mortgage) valuation.

Importantly, the constitution of this chain of valuation did not transpire through a linear progression, from control of the underwriting of mortgage-backed securities by government-sponsored enterprises (GSES), known as Freddie Mac and Fannie Mae, to freewheeling, free market private investment practices. As Poon insists (2009, 664), the shift from a system of rule-based rating to a system of score-based rating did not necessarily have to occur through FICO scores:

> The development of the subprime into a coherent network of mortgage finance in which securitization could take place was not a given. It would itself have to be materialized. To create a circuit of subprime finance would require a proliferation of specialized underwriting software equally grounded around and further reinforcing the use of the specific brand name credit scores elected and interpreted by the GSES. If at any moment another solution to evaluating consumer risk had been incorporated into private software when faced with the consumer, lenders would have produced a series of disconnected risk assessments. While this situation would not have precluded the emergence of subprime finance, it would have demanded a patchwork of solutions to the problem of commensuration, which would have complicated the calculative picture and, much like the previous system of letter grades, considerably weakened the transferability of risk into secondary markets. (Poon 2009, 664)[18]

The emergent control-by-risk regime was not overdetermined, or necessary to a form of capitalism or the hegemony of a particular kind of abstract value; it was a novel space of calculative possibility with a distinctive architecture, or manifestation, that can be empirically investigated as a living work—an oeuvre. In other words, "[The score scale] became a platform for creative design work that brought lines of risk calibrated products, both mortgages and securities, into existence. The introduction of a numerical scale of consumer credit quality into mortgage origination permitted calculative actions that were simply unanticipated from within the conventional frameworks of the GSES. This is how control-by-screening was concretely edged out in the non-GSE circuit by the productivity of credit-control-by-risk, whose characteristic is to act at the level of population, harnessing a variety of credit qualities through a proliferation of financial goods" (2009, 667). This account of credit scoring as a pragmatic analytics, giving rise to a novel chain of valuation, makes clear how *positive, pragmatic* spaces of calculative possibility bring about transformation.[19] No need for error or crisis.

Poon documents how the increasing transferability of risk results from the introduction of new organizational practices in the financial industry (see also Power 2007). She shows the emergence of risk as a particular commodity form, or how the value of high-risk loans was rendered stable enough for global exchange to occur, or for debt to be fungible, which implies agreement about the quality of aggregate forms. Credit risk was not simply an unregulated activity or product; it came to be a "firm expression" that was thus transferable across domains, making risk a product that gave rise to various markets, such as insurance against default and associated markets for these forms of insurance (credit default swaps, collateralized debt obligations).[20] Consumer mortgage debt was figured as an asset class that allowed for the creation of transferable debt. Poon's work helps to explain the very low level of investment activity in mortgage finance over the past fifty years, apart from the federally chartered prime investment market, which was due to the difficulty, during that time, of evaluating individual mortgage quality, or the difficulty of "stating credit risk as a firm expression *transferable across domains*" (2009, 666, my emphasis). Over the past several years, the productivity of risk has been generated and pursued through the practice of risk management models, the creation of market segments based on risk qualities, and the shorting of markets, or widespread bets "against the market" and "for" default, or *for* risk—all of which have been apprehended as a positive and effective means of wealth creation. We can now ask: How does a pragmatic analytics of risk, or of positive spaces of calculative possibility, serve alternative accounts of financial practice? If we don't ask "What went wrong?" then what questions do we ask?[21]

THE CRISIS THAT DOES NOT OBTAIN

Once crisis is posited, some questions are asked, others are foreclosed. Once crisis was pronounced, what was once taken to be an asset was deemed a toxic asset—what had been signified as a credit came to be signified as a debt. This transfiguration resulted from a judgment: the judgment "crisis," taken as a natural or historical systemic problem, a dissonance in truth value, a paradox. Little regard has been paid to the denotations, metrics, standards, differentiations, classifications, and observations that led to that very pronouncement. In our zealous rush to condemn unbridled greed and corruption, the freewheeling market, and groundless derivatives, little attention has been paid to the very practices that served a judgment that made possible and justified revaluation such that value was radically transformed through the massive expropriation of wealth and debt-driven recapitalization.

The declaration of crisis is a particular judgment. The massive devaluation that it justified most recently is usually spoken about through circumlocutory expressions. Nouriel Roubini, the well-known, self-described master of what he calls "Crisis Economics," uses several in one single interview (2010): "the re-leveraging of the public sector," "public-debt restructuring," and "socialization of part of the private sector's losses."[22] Not necessarily incorrect, since taxpayers were ushered in as the bankers of last resort (the "socialization" of private sector losses), these comments nevertheless shore up an analysis in terms of a systemic, naturalized process: de-leveraging, restructuring, socialization. Re-leveraging and devaluation are means to specific ends; they create particular effects (see Harvey 2003 on global imperialism, but see also Boas 1966 and Suttles 1968 on potlatch among the Kwakiutl of the Pacific Northwest coast). Through devaluation there is recapitalization: homes were lost to save banks. Here we can see how the declaration of "crisis" is a distinction that produces meaning: there is (now) dissonance between true value and representations of that value. This information becomes the very grounds for devaluation and recapitalization.

In this way, we "capitalize on crisis." This expression, coined by Greta Krippner (2011) in her carefully researched book, *Capitalizing on Crisis*, refers to state efforts to secure the extension of credit through domestic and global capital markets so as to resolve perceived domestic political dilemmas regarding economic distribution or resource allocation. In that sense, Krippner's account replaces the "deregulation then crisis" narrative with "crisis then deregulation."[23] She first posits moments of successive crisis (social, fiscal, legitimation) and then proceeds to investigate policy decisions that led to the "capitalization of crisis." Crisis here serves as an a priori: Krippner assumes that crisis (social or political) exists, which then incites the state to capitalization, most distinctly through financial institutions. This assumption is reminiscent of what Peter Osborne (2010, 23) calls "the Weberian methodological turn in crisis theory," which pluralizes forms of crisis as a remedy to the economic determinism implied by Marxist accounts of the permanent tendency for crisis inherent to the capitalist mode of production. This socialization of the notion of economic crisis has been construed most notably by Jürgen Habermas as "legitimation crisis." Following in the prints of this typological approach, Krippner takes crisis for granted: it is the fixed point from which she begins her narration; and it is a means to account for the emergent, which, for her study, is the process of financialization or the inception of political-economic regulatory regimes. However, as she herself indicates throughout her book, hers is an account of averted crises: through a series of financial and institutional innovations, repeatedly, the dread meltdown never occurs and political dilemmas consistently are deferred or suspended.[24] Effectively, crisis never obtains.

Similarly, one dread meltdown was evidently averted in September 2008, when the United States Federal Reserve announced a guarantee of money market accounts. Supposedly, or as Democratic congressman Paul Kanjorski, chairman of the Capital Markets Subcommittee, presaged, "If they had not done that, their estimation is that by 2 p.m. that afternoon $5.5 trillion would have been drawn out of the money-market system of the US; [this] would have collapsed the entire economy of the US, and within 24 hours the world economy would have collapsed. It would have been the end of our economic system and our political system as we know it." Ben Bernanke, chairman of the Federal Reserve, further validated this apocalyptic vision and recourse to the comprehensive bailout plan by warning Congress on Thursday, September 18: "We may not have an economy on Monday" (both quoted in Skidelsky 2009, 9–10).[25]

What does it mean to "not have an economy"? And what is signified by the "collapse of the world economy"? It seems possible that private banks could go bankrupt but that humans would still have an economy. It seems possible that the private banking system as we know it could lose its capital but that public or political provisions could be made for citizens to not be divested of an economy.[26] But recent crisis narratives portended the end of our political-economic system as we know it; the very claim to crisis entailed distinctions that gave meaning to "socialized private sector losses," that gave reason to the capitalization of private markets through public debt, and that ultimately made crisis the *ever-elusive* horizon of a future.

Some might protest: but crisis obtained for homeowners. People lost their homes; the value of the homes they continued to inhabit was deemed nil; they lost their jobs and could not pay their rent; they lost retirement pensions and could not find jobs to pay their mortgages or their rent—they were rendered insolvent. As Randy Martin (2009) puts it so aptly: "Whose Crisis Is That?" Other observers similarly raise this question of distributive justice. Presaging the Occupy Wall Street movement, Greta Krippner (2011, 139) reads the history of crisis as a function of the everlasting question: "Which social actors should bear the burden of a fading prosperity?" In her view, the recent and recurring history of financialization merely defers this question because it suspends distributional conflict. She concludes that financialization can no longer serve the purpose of temporarily resolving problems of resource allocation, gesturing, rather hopefully, to a post-finance future (see also Fligstein 2005). Writing prior to the emergence of Occupy Wall Street, she attributes the lack of a crisis-inspired social movement—rising, for instance, from a coalition of middle-class homeowners and urban-based consumer advocates—to the depoliticization of conflict over resource allocation, which is facilitated through recourse to the market and finance (Krippner 2011, 82–85 and 144; see also Martin 2009). In David Harvey's view (2011), with equal hope, compound growth can no longer serve as an effective manner of organizing the global political economy. He sees the lack of a broad-based anticapitalist movement, which would bring in step environmentalists, anarchists, NGOs, traditional leftist parties, trade unions, and *altermondialistes,* as a problem of devising adequate organizational forms that would neither be subsumed by abstract principles, such as exclusionary rules of organization, nor amount to a motley of methods (Harvey 2011, 110–12).

These extremely worthy viewpoints are not betrayed by the (ephemeral?) appearance of Occupy movements across the globe. That is, ultimately, questions raised regarding socioeconomic distribution and the prospects for social movements that articulate critique by-pass entirely a constitutive aspect of such change: the very question, which social actors should bear the burden of a fading prosperity? has not been transformed or rendered illegible. Despite claims to the end of finance as we know it, the end of financialization, the end of an imperial hegemonic structure, we have not achieved the "new times" of crisis. We still ask the same questions. They remain valid propositions for the scheme of oppositions and binaries (capital versus labor, use value versus surplus value, politics versus morality) through which we reason. Eventually, questions must be devised that address the *status of these propositions.* Instead of acceding to crisis—instead of presuming its status as foundational to historical events and historical transformation—and thus assuming that what is at stake is re-source allocation or income distribution, we might step back to consider *what is at stake with crisis in-and-of-itself.*

Contemporary accounts of crisis take as their subject the *politics of crisis*; they elaborate critique in terms of ideological and political failure. Although such scholarship no longer vaunts confidence in the teleological nature of time and events, or a philosophy of history, diagnoses of ideological and political failure necessarily imply a certain telos—that is, they are inevitably, though most often implicitly, directed toward a norm. Critique is predicated on crisis, which is mobilized in these narrative forms as an organic analogy. The telos implied by this form of critique is implicit because, as an organic analogy, crisis does not imply, in itself, a definite direction of change, nor does it predict an outcome—a point made most clearly by Randolph Starn (1971), one of the few historians to raise the question of the epistemological status of crisis as an object of historiography.[27] Crisis is a narrative device: "Applied to any place or period, it may assuage the historian's usual discomfort with extremes, allowing him to have both continuity and change, for 'crisis' implies the continuity of organic processes but not steady equilibrium, decisive conflict but not 'total' revolution" (Starn 1971, 17).[28] Recourse to "crisis" as a narrative device seems to preserve conditions of radical contingency, but it also serves a philosophy of history insofar as it entails reflection on the meaning of events (even if one particular narrative of events is not privileged); it demonstrates, by serializing events, that one set of events was logical (the conditions of possibility of a particular history); and it selects or privileges both events and series of events on the basis of particular epistemological criteria, and hence eradicates contingency (Munz 1977, 295–97).[29]

Beyond the discomforts of historians, the French philosopher and logician Daniel Parrochia sums up this state of affairs, or the privileging of "the event," for contemporary social science succinctly:

> From a philosophical point of view, during the last quarter of the century we have witnessed perhaps not "the end of History" but at least the end of philosophies of history, if by that we mean mes-

sianic belief systems that entail an unyielding confidence in a teleology of time. Whether it be the Christian eschatology of a para-
disiacal community; the Enlightenment belief in the irreversible
progress of humanity towards happiness and "perfect health"; the
Communist vision of a pacified, classless society; or even the recent utopia of a world of perfectly transparent communication—all
are versions (religious or secular) of a "becoming" (*un devenir*) that
is oriented toward a collective imaginary. What remains, it seems,
for these majestic manners of organizing shared time is a pointed
attention to *events*. The latter constitute, in their often irruptive
nature, the elements of a network, the signification of which is
not preordained and which must be reconstituted patiently, like a
puzzle or a painting that has no model. (2008, 5–6, my translation)

To be sure, recourse to "moments" ("the postcolonial moment"),
events, and networks does indeed characterize the constitutive elements of contemporary social science narratives, being a reflection
of strategies for avoiding teleology. Crisis figures as an element in
that constellation of concepts; its increasingly widespread use is in
part a symptom of such strategies.[30] Thus an entire array of institutions, situations, and processes—the nation-state, humanitarianism,
war, migration, empire, citizenship, finance capital—have been interpreted with reference to "crisis," "states of exception," and "states
of emergency" as the fundamental conditions of their emergence.[31]
"Risk," "catastrophe," "disaster," "emergency," "crisis," "trauma,"
"shock"—these are rapidly proliferating nouns (often used as adjec-
tives: "disaster capitalism") in a great deal of writing today. Some of
this work is dedicated to exploring the very emergence of such critical situations. For example, as reviewed above, much compelling
work demonstrates the emergence of "financialization" as a generalized form of wealth production, now spanning both nonfinancial and
financial domains of life. Some of this work relates to "the politics
of crisis," taking crisis to be a contested term and thus joining the
ranks of writing on the apparent states of the contemporary world
(see Martin 2010b on financialization; Franklin 1998 on the politics
of risk society; Jasanoff 1994 on the politics of disaster; Steinmetz

2003 on the politics of emergency; and Fassin and Pandolfi 2010 on the politics of humanitarian crisis). In these explorations of the politics of crisis, it is typically assumed that, while contested and an object of various forms of politics, crisis is an object of empirical knowledge. The grounds for such knowledge are left unexamined: crisis is a condition of human history and human affairs. Crises happen and crises are propagated; they *then* become sites of contestation, with political and social consequences. Crisis—be it disputed, contested, authored—has a particular status in history.

In keeping with this assumption regarding the empirical status of crisis, Daniel Parrochia calls for an "urgent reflection" on crises as empirical events because, despite the end of philosophies of history, history itself is nevertheless accessible to rationality. Crisis events are privileged entry points into the logics or rationalities of history: crisis translates empirical specificity into the language of generality, understood as trends, topologies, probabilities, and logical-mathematical models. Parrochia's quest to recuperate history for rationality is in some ways reminiscent of past claims for the fulfillment of the demands of reason, or the assumption and desire to demonstrate that "change takes place in analogous forms" (Koselleck 2002, 240). But his project is in keeping with a recent trend that admits of an ontological condition of uncertainty and nonetheless takes up the problem of rationality as a matter of pure logic:

> The absence of finalities does not mean renunciation, and the inescapable presence of both chance (*le hasard*) and the "logic of a grain of sand"[32] is by no means crippling. The very existence of powerful logical-mathematical models—be it in the domain of differential topology or probability or game theory or graphics—should allow us to restore explanatory associations (*filiations explicatives*) and give reasons to hope. We should keep ourselves, nonetheless, from creating new myths. A general theory of crises remains to be established. (Parrochia 2008, 7, my translation)

The theorization of crises would be a science of change; it would be a victory of reason over contingency. This is, of course, an ancient battle, as Parrochia acknowledges:

To be sure, Hegelian philosophy had the incomparable merit of demonstrating how speculative thought (*la pensée speculative*) could overcome contingency, but this was at the price of a transformation in the image of reason, which became divine Reason — that is to say, *Dé-raison*, *Sur-raison* and *Trans-raison*, all at once. A return to the real presupposes, then, not only effective recognition of the power of chance (*le hasard*), but also the possibility of its mathematical determination, be that in the form of the mastery of randomness via the theory of probability or in the diverse forms of the mathematics of action (game theory, simulation, etc.). In this context, but only in this context, we affirm the possibility of a theory of crises and the new vision of time that it carries with it. (2008, 12, my translation)[33]

Parrochia hopes to bridge the epistemological divide between empiricism and pure logic. He warns against oppositions between history, on the one hand, and "the rational understanding of conflicts and crises," on the other, quoting, somewhat cryptically, the French philosopher Augustin Cournot, who sets forth the anecdotal facts that precipitated a general crisis: "the grain of sand in Cromwell's urethra, the gust of wind that kept the Prince of Orange in the waters of Zealand or that brought him to Toray, Lady Churchill's glass of water that saved the works of Richelieu and the great king" (quoted in 2008, 19). His point is that one must distinguish between "causes" and "reasons," or between empirical causality and reason in/of history. The role of chance (*le hasard*) — the combination or the fortuitous encounter of events belonging, respectively, to independent series — in history and in nature is, as Cournot maintained, fundamental and precludes any deterministic causal theory of history. However, there are "laws of chance" in the mathematical sense. While we cannot aspire to knowledge of the laws of history, we can hope to establish laws of probability with regard to history. For Parrochia, history is still accessible to reason and the entryway is crisis, which is endowed with a foundational status and revelatory role. He therefore maintains that "every crisis is in reality revelatory of a conflict, which is doubtless latent at the onset, but which becomes, through the crisis, exacerbated" (33). And he concludes that, because "man is in permanent tension with his environment (*milieu*), [he] is naturally inclined to existential conflict. But the latter reveals itself only in times of crisis" (34).[34]

For Parrochia, the concept of crisis is the point of departure for the regeneration of a philosophy of history grounded in the laws of probability as opposed to the Law of History because crisis is a revelatory moment—an "event" in historical time as well as an "event" that is the disclosure of the existential conditions of life.[35] This claim for the foundational status of crisis that seeks to reinvigorate the history of rationality elides the ways in which crisis entails judgment: judging time in terms of analogous intervals and judging history in terms of its significance. Here again, the question remains: what is the burden of proof for such judgment? The existential conflict that Parrochia diagnoses as the symptom of dissonance—man in tension with his environment—denotes a familiar story of alienation: the historical significance of this tension is revealed to us via crisis. In Parrochia's formulation, historical significance can be apprehended at the level of structure (specifically, logical-mathematical structure). In his hope to ascertain the laws of probability with regard to history, Parrochia explores the limits of intelligibility and yet also seeks the grounds for knowledge of historical significance with regard to the future.

The moral demand for a future—a future free of capitalist imperial expansion, a future divested of the logics of compound growth, a future constructed out of the differential ability to anticipate and regulate, a future mastered through the power of chance—is a demand for, in Koselleck's words (2002, 250), "redemption within history or the negation of alienation." One might share the desire for an end to capitalist imperial expansion and the end of compound growth as the basis for value, and yet still raise the question of whether or not such a demand could be formulated without discerning historical significance in terms of human error, in terms of ethical failure. Can we narrate a future without crisis? An answer to that question might imply that we somehow obliterate the strange idea that history can be alienated in terms of its philosophy, or that we can perceive of a dissonance between historical events and representations of those events. How can we imagine that which fundamentally excludes our judgment, that which calls for no decision?[36] Contemporary claims to crisis are the grounds for the critique of capitalism, the critique of imperialism, the critique of the efficient market hypothesis, the critique of the politics of crisis, but they are not the grounds for alternative narratives or for other histories. The judgment of crisis is a distinction that produces information, which serves to reproduce existing dichotomies and extant hierarchies: public-private, economy-society, morality-politics, material-ideal, and so forth.

DREAMS

William Rasch sums up our dilemma concisely: "We have become distinctly suspicious of transcendental attempts to construct inviolate and panoramic levels of vision labeled God, Reason, or Truth. Yet, because of political or moral commitments, we are equally disinclined to relinquish 'critical' perspectives from which we presume not only to see the world as it is but also to utter judgments about its inadequacy" (2000, 127). Even if a critical perspective is relegated to provisional ends, and thus applies itself to "bearing witness" to difference and partial interests, these exclusions (the Other, the silenced, the non-sovereign, the dispossessed, etc.) are apprehended in terms of negative integration.[1] The reflexive stance, which recognizes the contingency of its observations and accounts for the ways that the observer itself constructs its object of investigation, has similar implications. It means that the various disciplines of the social sciences are no longer defined by their object of inquiry: sociology is for the most part no longer the positivistic study of "society," and ethnography is for the most part no longer the positivistic study of "the ethnos." In the place of disciplinary objects, we have constitutive questions.[2] The obvious constitutive question is framed in terms of the conditions of possibility for a given situation, practice, institution, et cetera. The less obvious but equally pervasive constitutive question is, what went wrong?

That question brings us back to the matter, raised above, of what is expected of history—that is, the moral demand for a difference between past and future. Doubtless the world could be otherwise; we can envisage amendments that would address poverty and well-being. But the movements or publics that emerge around these very issues must be acknowledged as such—that is, acknowledged as movements for self-determination or as autonomously constituted publics with recognized and legitimated claims to rights. It is not clear that such publics constitute an alternative politics because they are inevitably inscribed in, for example, the language of rights and sovereignty. As Foucault maintained in an overly quoted passage, "The important thing here, I believe, is that truth isn't outside power, or lacking in power . . . truth isn't the reward of free spirits, the child of protracted solitude, nor the privilege of those who have succeeded in liberating themselves. Truth is a thing of this world produced only by virtue of multiple forms of constraint. . . . 'Truth' is to be understood as a system of *ordered procedures for the production, regulation, distribution, circulation and operation of statements*" (Foucault 1980, 131). Moreover, as Koselleck argued in his presentation of the private, secret Masonic lodges, political legitimacy is generated out of the supposed exile of moral innocence, out of hypocrisy. Or, in Luhmann's words, "The secret of alternative movements is that they cannot offer any alternatives" (1990b, 141).[3] *Without a non-foundational foundation for political action, we can only have crisis and anti-crisis, not crisis and something else.*

Taking issue with the guiding question that drives our construction of history from a negative formulation—what went wrong?—does not amount to a denial of error, or the "acts and omissions of mankind" (Koselleck 2006, 371). I have merely trained my sights elsewhere so as to think about how the term "crisis" operates as a non-place in the formulation of that question and in possible replies. Because the historical significance of our contemporary situation is construed in terms of systemic, structural, or moral failure, answers to the question, what went wrong? are necessarily sought in latencies that account for error: for instance, in the classic cases of Marxism and psychoanalysis, respectively, class interest accounts for ideology and traumatic experience accounts for pathological behavior (cf. Rasch 2002, 3). The proverbial problem is to apprehend these systems or deeper structures from a vantage point that is not itself determined by them. Crisis often serves to signify such a vantage point, especially in accounts that seek to determine the "mediations" that might exist between structural crisis and experiential crisis, or between crisis as a descriptive category and crisis as an evaluative category (cf. Habermas 1975; Benhabib 1986). This manner of "reading off" surface contingencies as symptomatic of a totalizing secular prime mover (capitalism, consciousness) has been taken to task over and again. But the way that "crisis" serves as a non-locus from which to signify such contingencies in the first place has not been the object of much thought.

As a non-locus for signifying contingency, crisis is not a diagnostic of history as such. Under the sign of crisis, "events" are distinguished and signified; they achieve empirical status as "history" and hence become legible to us. Crisis partakes of a metaphysics of history: consequently, Obama's witnessing, or his judgment of moral significance as being located in history and as being the stuff of history itself. In marking out a "moment of truth" in this way, certain questions can be asked while others are foreclosed. In his case, the referenced "historical crisis" is the subprime mortgage market for which answers to the question, what went wrong? have been located either in the systemic nature of capitalism (the business cycle, the falling rate of profit) or in the moral failings of speculative finance capital (producing "bubbles" of false value). These interpretations avoid examination of the ways in which crisis is not intrinsic to a system or the result of a teleology, but is rather a distinction that produces meaning. Thus, for example, the massive devaluation of real estate values (versus their "natural" tendency to diminish) resulted in a tide of home foreclosures, which was seen as the natural result of an insufficiently collateralized debt market. The decision by the banking industry and the American government to define economic conditions in terms of crisis at a particular moment remains an unambiguous, unchallenged judgment. Naming this situation "crisis" implies that what was once perfectly intelligible and construed as productive (debt is a credit) is now taken to be without basis and construed as a negative value form (debt is a toxic asset).

Answers to the question, what went wrong? are devised according to the "is" versus "ought" distinctions inherent to paradox. This means that post hoc analyses in terms of crisis necessarily entail an assumed teleology. To continue with the recent case of subprime mortgages, these assessments entail assumptions about how "the market" *should* function and conjecture about how deviations from "true" market value were produced. These judgments do not account for the ways in which such value results from coordinated modes of evaluation and calculation, which are not merely the product of the law of capitalism or the law of the market; they arise from specific technical practices, such as underwriting, accounting, and risk management, allowing debt to be figured as a fungible asset. Reference to "financial crisis" with respect to the subprime mortgage market only serves to unify the disparate modes of evaluation that are essential to the coordination of specific chains of valuation and calculation, which merit systematic study. In eliding such study, reference to "crisis" can only identify the historical significance of the contemporary situation in terms of systemic and ethical failures.[4]

But crisis narratives are not "false," nor are they mere representations, to be compared to a truer narrative or a more solid level underlying mere symbolic terrain. It follows that the aim is not to invalidate "crisis" or to critique the term as inaccurate or merely symbolic. There is no reason to claim that there are no "real" crises. Rather, the point is to observe crisis as a blind spot, and hence to apprehend the ways in which it regulates narrative constructions, the ways in which it allows certain questions to be asked while others are foreclosed.[5] In that sense, there is no need for unconditional skepticism or nihilism.[6] Rather than devotion to reconciling such paradox, or antinomies, one might prefer to consider what it would take to "reconcile *ourselves* to the *inevitability* of antinomies" (Rasch 2000, 9, emphasis in original). With contingency serving as the transcendental placeholder, having usurped both God and reason, we have no choice but to ground our faith in it—or in crisis, ultimately a signifier for contingency—via the

"the series of stories" that are written, or more to the point, "in the very necessity of having to write stories" (Rasch 2000, 23).

The problem of narrative and representation is obviously not new; it is a central dilemma of the social sciences.[7] At least for now, the endeavor to put forth forms of nonrepresentational thinking, and nonnarrative forms of memory and rationality, most often inspired by Gilles Deleuze, Jacques Derrida or, more recently, Henri Bergson, are nevertheless presented in narrative form.[8] For as long as the "necessity of having to write stories" remains compelling, rather than (somewhat ironically) writing books to banish narrativity, we could ask: "what form should this writing, thinking, and inquiring take? And to what telos does it strive?" (Rabinow 2008, 49). These are the questions I put to crisis narratives. If the concept of crisis presently serves as a noun-formation of contemporary historical narrative, and if, despite its cognate status to critique, it serves to enshrine and reinstitute long-standing and enduring principles, as I have maintained herein, then we should take thoughtful consideration of Paul Rabinow's suggestion: "I am advocating the pursuit of a *larger series of limited concepts*. Why? Because if, as philosophically oriented anthropologists, the goal of our labor is understanding, then our concepts and our modes of work must themselves be capable of *making something new happen* in a field of knowledge" (1999, 182, my emphasis).[9] Those limited concepts cannot be known a priori, of course; they emerge, are articulated, and are crafted through inquiry.[10] This form of inquiry requires the abandonment of epochal thinking, as described above; it is inquiry into "what is taking place without deducing it beforehand" (Rabinow 2008, 2–3). Most significantly, such inquiry must be self-conscious in its distinctions: what if inquiry proceeded from a different set of distinctions? One guiding question for inquiry would be: "What if we did not begin with the distinction between a whole to be captured and an inquiring subject to be rendered transparent? . . . What then would observation consist in?" (2008, 54).[11]

One might ask: what sort of narrative could be produced where meaning is not everywhere a problem?[12] If history amounts to a record of interruptions (suffering, alienation, crisis) how does one successfully resist or avoid the temptation to achieve admission into the record, thus severing recognition and noteworthiness from the achievement of politics?[13] In the end, this politics would entail a true epistemological revolution because significance would no longer be located in history. Martin Luther King Jr. never pronounced "Normalcy—Never Again": there is no politics without crisis.[14] Or this would be an impractical, impossible politics whose form we could not imagine, since it would presumably somehow, someway subvert the temporalization of history. Instead, Martin Luther King Jr. pronounced "I Have a Dream," reinscribing his politics in hope for the future, in a politics of redemption—a politics of hope that was restated resoundingly by Barack Obama on the National Mall. The problem is the future: "With the discovery that the time of history was different from the time of nature, man also came to believe that historical time could be affected by human action and purposiveness in ways that natural time could not, that history could be 'made' as well as 'suffered,' and that a historical knowledge true to its 'concept' provided the prospects for a science of society that balanced the claims of experience with the insistencies of expectation, hope, and faith in the future" (White 2002, xi).

In the words of Umberto Eco, reflecting upon the *narrative paradox* of political-action-packed Superman: "Time as a *structure of possibility* is, in fact, the problem of our moving toward a future" (Eco 1984, 112, emphasis in original). Eco is fascinated with narrativity in Superman, in which, through multiple, truncated and nested trajectories; flashes, reversals, setbacks, duplications, parallels, recurrences, and reprises, the concept of time breaks down: events lose a notion of temporal progression, as in a dream.[15] But a dream, surely just like history, is "a cosmically unnoticeable event" (Blumenberg 1997, 38): there is no spectator, no witness.[16] No Inauguration Day.

NOTES

INTRODUCTION: WHAT IS AT STAKE?

1. The various "Normalcy—Never Again" drafts, the final text penned by Martin Luther King Jr., and conjecture about his reasons for deviating from the prepared speech can be found in Hansen 2005.

2. "Transcript: Barack Obama's Inaugural Address," delivered January 20, 2009, Washington, DC, accessed January 20, 2009, http://ww.npr.org/templates/story>php?storyId=99590481&ps=cprs.

3. This book is not intended as an exhaustive account of the social science literature and will be primarily concerned with contemporary narrations of "financial crisis."

4. Starn (1971) and Beckett (2008) undertake two helpful reviews of the term "crisis." Starn considers the epistemological status of crisis in the tradition of Western academic historiography. Beckett shows how crisis has been thematized in Haiti in relation to a wider discursive field in which the notion of "decline" is dependent upon ideas of progress held to obtain outside of Haiti, most notably in the global North. See also Parrochia 2008 and Shank 2008, both of which review the concept of crisis for social science theory and historical studies, respectively.

5. Referencing this bibliography would take up an inordinate amount of space, as would the notation of recent conferences dedicated to "explaining the crisis," impulsively staged by universities, think tanks, and periodicals. The extensive bibliography on contemporary "financial crisis" is referenced below. For a fascinating screen-based art installation on the term "crisis," which uses live news feeds, data processing, and typographical imagery to visualize how the replication of the term generates—and does not merely reflect—a particu-

lar situation, see Katie Levitt's *Poetical Crisis*, http://katielevitt.wordpress.com accessed March 25, 2008.

6. This project started with Africa in 2006. At that time, financial crisis was not my object of thought. The question I put to myself was: how can one think about Africa—or think "Africa"—otherwise than under the sign of crisis? As I have written elsewhere (Roitman forthcoming), although the African continent is designated and conjured under the sign of crisis, this is not a diagnostic of a continent. It is a diagnostic of history as such. In the same way that our contemporary history is qualified as humanitarian crisis, environmental crisis, financial crisis, et cetera, and is thus given ontological status as "history" through these terms, "Africa" is posited as an ontological category of thought under the sign of crisis.

7. A full bibliography of these literatures is noted below. I am using "2007–9" as an indicator, referencing the "financial crisis" referred to by Barack Obama, or what is sometimes more specifically called the "subprime mortgage crisis," even though some of this literature was produced slightly before or after that time period.

8. Rabinow is interested in designing inquiry. He does not take anthropology to be "ethnography understood as a practice developed to analyze a specific type of object—the culture and/or society of *ethnoi*—so as to contribute to a specific genre, the monograph (or journal article)." Instead, the practice of anthropology entails "the dynamic and mutually constitutive, if partial . . . , connections between figures of *anthropos* and the diverse, and at times inconsistent, branches of knowledge available during a period of time; that claim authority about the truth of the matter; and whose legitimacy to make such claims is accepted as plausible by other such claimants; as well as the power relations within which and through which those claims are produced, established, contested, defeated, affirmed, and disseminated" (2008, 4). It should be noted that Rabinow refers to a disjuncture between "the moral landscape inhabited in daily life" and "the moral landscape as reflected upon by those authorized to pronounce prescriptive speech acts about it" (2008, 79). However, he also underscores the complex subject positions of his "natives," such as molecular biologists working on genome mapping who are likewise practicing Christians or scientists of a molecular science laboratory who hold credence in the category of "race." The object of inquiry is the ethical practices entailed by such lives. And in the process of that inquiry, one is adjacent to both the "universal intellectual" typical to the academy and the "specific intellectual," who inhabits expert worlds (see 33–50). Cf. Rabinow 2003.

9. This statement summarizes various ways of construing the possibility for and aims of critique, which are spelled out with reference to specific scholars, in chapter 1.

10. See Rasch 2000 and 2002.

11. For Luhmann, this necessarily contingent world is signified by the term "modernity." Though characterized by the "loss of an outside," or loss of an outside reference point, Luhmann does not see this situation of necessary contingency as a problem, or a loss to be lamented or condemned. Cf. Luhmann [1992] 1998, 2002; and Rasch 2000. Though he does not consider the term "crisis," my thinking is inspired by the work of Niklas Luhmann, discussed below.

12. This statement smacks of an idealist or constructivist position, which states that there is no knowledge-independent reality. See 37–39 of this book for clarification. In particular, at least for my rendering of crisis as a logical observation, see Luhmann 1990a; Christis 2001; and Rasch 2012. But more generally, cf. Rorty 1979; Bernstein 1983; Hacking 1999; Latour 2003; and Meillassoux 2008, among others.

13. The concept of a philosophy of history denotes the process necessary for the narration of the passage of time as history, which abides a selection principle that distinguishes between reality and an account of reality. See 22–31 of this book; and refer to White 1973 and Munz 1977.

14. This notion of observation, inspired by Luhmann, is developed below. In a review of the influence of Spencer Brown and Foerster on Luhmann, Jac Christis (2001, 334) states this quite plainly: "So, on the first level, observers simply observe (a table). No observer can observe how he observes (the distinction between table and chair) at the same time as he observes what he observes. Only in a second-order observation can we indicate the distinction used in a first-order observation. This obviously means that the 'how' of a first-order observation becomes the 'what' of a second-order observation." See also Fuchs 1996, 323, cited by Christis. Luhmann's point is not that all first-order operations are empirical, as in a radical empiricist's view. Observation is a matter of fundamental contingency: "Observation is any kind of operation that makes a distinction so as to designate one (but not the other) side. Such a definition is itself contingent, since what is defined would have another meaning given another distinction" (1998, 47). "The real" is what is practiced as a distinction (see chapter 1, 37–39) and the contingent nature of first-order operations is not problematic; one can note, quite simply, that any first-order observation can be qualified as contingent *by a second-order observer*, ad infinitum.

15. The mere act of posing these questions is a form of critique insofar as the formulation of a question potentially posits the possible limits of knowledge. Though not focusing on that elusive category "power," I nonetheless take up Judith Butler's question (2002, 214): "What is the relation of knowledge to power such that our epistemological certainties turn out to support a way of structuring the world that forecloses alternative possibilities of ordering?" In that sense, my practice of critique follows in the steps of Michel Foucault and Judith Butler, as presented below. But, as we will see below, for both Foucault

and Butler, as for others, this form of critique entails or even necessitates crisis. So while not "against" this practice of critique, I am noting how it posits crisis as an a priori. See 34, this book.

16. David Bloor's expression is apt for my own project; his concern, however, is the sociology of knowledge (Bloor 1991, 2001). For debate over his position, see the exchange between Bloor and Latour: Bloor 1999a, 1999b; Latour 1999a.

17. The very possibility of observation presupposes conditions of observation, which themselves are not observable. All observations or points of view entail blind spots, insofar as there can never be an observation, cognition, or knowledge of a totality. In that sense, all observations, cognitions, or points of view have blind spots, which, when made visible from another perspective, are reproduced ad infinitum.

18. In his reflective essay on Husserl's *Crisis of the European Sciences* ([1954] 1970), James Dodd (2004, 19) notes similar questions, though with the aim, following Husserl, to show that science itself would not be possible without a human understanding of the world as a problem, or experienced as failure.

1. CRISIS DEMANDS

1. I use the plural (histories) to underscore the heterogeneity of any possible genealogy. With respect to Koselleck's particular historiography, see Davis 2008 and note 28 in this chapter. Many thanks to Gil Anidjar for referring me to her work.

2. See the eight-volume work edited by Brunner, Conze, and Koselleck (1972–97). Koselleck's extensive writing on this subject and on the ultimate question of the emergence of *Neuzeit* (the modern age, modernity) as a historical concept has been commented on at length. I will not reappraise his body of work or contribute to the secondary literature. For brief reviews, cf. Tribe 1989 and Richter 1990. The main body of Koselleck's work in English includes Koselleck 1988 [original German 1959], 2002, 2004 [original German 1979]. While beyond the scope of this essay, one might note the influence of Hegel, Husserl, Gadamer, Schmitt, and Heidegger on Koselleck with respect to his hermeneutic approach and the "presence of the future," all of which can be explored in, for example, Tribe 1989; Hoffmeyer 1994; Palonen 1999; Palti 2010. See also Blumenberg 1997 and 2010.

3. This is a simplified presentation of Koselleck's portrayal of the mutually constituted possibilities of past, present, and future; and the extent to which the lived present is necessarily a "former future," all of which indicates the influence of Heidegger on Koselleck's thinking, especially as presented in the publication *Futures Past*. See Carr 1987.

4. Koselleck goes so far as to assert that crisis is necessary for the art of progno-

sis, which he defines as a structural analysis that gives rise to "metahistorical statements in which the conditions of possible histories and thus of possible futures are reflected" (2002, 145).

5. For his conceptual history of crisis, see Koselleck [1959] 1988, [1972–97] 2006, [1979] 2004, and 2002. The numerous texts in German are found in Koselleck's bibliography (cf. notably 2006). For short articles that offer encyclopedia-style entries on the term "crisis," cf. Starn 1971; Masur 1973; Béjin and Morin 1976.

6. According to Koselleck, in Aristotle's *Politics*, crisis signifies a decision insofar as it implies a verdict or a judgment. And as a legal code, crisis was at the heart of the civic ordering of the community; only citizens could be judges, meaning that crisis, as decision and judgment, was constitutive of the civic community and was a means for establishing justice and good order. This juridical sense is incorporated into the Greek translation of the Old and New Testaments (*Septuaginta*). See Koselleck's detailed account (2006, 359), where he likewise notes (361) that the adoption of the term in Latin contributed to its metaphorical extension, rendering it a transitional and temporal concept.

7. It is important to note that, for Koselleck's brand of conceptual history, and contrary to a history of ideas, concepts cannot be defined; they have no inner core meaning that undergoes permutations. Instead, concepts consist of semantic webs of meaning, which bring definitions into a wider relational nexus, thus producing relatively stable units of sense. Cf. Koselleck [1979] 2004, 75–92. The various "semantic options" are set forth as distinct but not mutually exclusive in 2002, 240–44, and 2006, 371–72.

8. By a European concept of history, I refer to the project of *Geschictliche Grundbegriffe*.

9. Read also Koselleck 2004, esp. chapter 13. His argument is greatly indebted to Löwith (1949), who demonstrates the Judeo-Christian eschatological framework underlying certain historical concepts, such as progress, as well as to Schmitt ([1922] 1985) regarding the transposition of theological forms to modern jurisprudence and to the political form of the modern state, through which theology becomes immanent. The influence of Schmitt and Löwith on Koselleck is determining; although there are significant differences in their positions on the extension of Christianity, or Western Christiandom (Anidjar 2006), all share an interest in the politicization of religious ideals and terms, with an eye to the ultimate question of political legitimacy. For a differing view, cf. Blumenberg 1997.

10. For another account of this temporalization see Lovejoy [1936] 1976.

11. According to Koselleck (2006, 360, and footnote 10 in that work), although the Last Judgment is yet to come, the Annunciation makes this cosmic event of future historical time already present as the Christian conscience. Following Löwith and Schmitt, Kathleen Davis rightly contests Koselleck's portrayal

of medieval stasis: "Despite Koselleck's intense focus on a Christian theology, his version of premodern untemporalized history never acknowledges the earlier periodization instantiated by the incarnation—that is, the temporal logic whereby Christianity subsumed and superseded Jewish history—as it had been explicated, for instance, by Löwith" (2008, 92). She refers to Biddick (2003), who notes the core role of "the Christian conception of supersession" in secularization narratives. And she illustrates how, for Koselleck, "politics," or "rational foresight," breaks the "cyclic grip of prophecy." She thus affirms Schmitt's refutation of the "eschatological, atemporal paralysis that Koselleck attributes to the Middle Ages" (93).

12. Koselleck claims that one cannot underestimate the influence of Leibniz's metaphysics for the emergence of this form of prognosis.

13. On crisis, prognosis, and knowledge of past and future, see Koselleck 2004, chapters 1 and 9. Koselleck in effect documents diminishing Aristotelian semantic content during what he defines as a "saddle period" (1750–1850), after which terms such as democracy, freedom, and progress entail a novel "anticipatory content" (2002, 5). Both Koselleck (2002, 167) and Blumenberg (1997, 58) make reference to Goethe with regard to this temporal shift in experience and his critique of the philosophy of history in terms of progress. See also Blumenberg (1997, 87) on Kant's assertion that time is not a discursive concept, but rather an a priori form, which he relates to the claim, made subsequently by both Koselleck and Blumenberg, that spatial representation is an older form than temporal representation. But see especially Löwith, who disavows this claim that "modern historical thinking begins only in modern times, with the eighteenth century" (1949, 2). Overall, these positions regarding transitions and the emergence of new forms of temporal experience must be read as political acts of periodization, an argument made by Davis (2008). Ideally, my exploration of the term "crisis" in social science narrative would elaborate on the subject of temporality more fully, with reference to Cohn [1896] 1994; Koyre 1957; Bender and Wellbery 1991; Ermarth 1992; Adam 1995, 2004; Osborne 1995; Butterfield 1999; Grosz 1999; May and Thrift 2001; Doane 2002; Le Poidevin 2003, 2007; Nowotny 2005; and Hoy 2009.

14. One of the main features of the historical concept of *Neuzeit* is the assumption that "time is always new," insofar as "every present differentiates itself from every past and every future; it is unique and therefore new" (Koselleck 2002, 148). *Neuzeit* entails an open future. Of course, Koselleck's analysis of *Neuzeit* echoes those of other authors; they will not be commented on, since my aim is to explore his presentation of the temporalization of history as it relates to his history of the concept of crisis. It is worth noting that his analysis of the linguistic usage of the term *perfectio* (perfectibility, as a finite goal) through the eighteenth century illustrates the way in which the future had been apprehended not as a dimension of progress, but rather as the end

of the world, the signs of which were constantly pursued and identified. See especially 2002, chapter 13; and see Koselleck's conceptual history of the term "progress" and his analysis of "acceleration" as the defining characteristic of *Neuzeit*. On the emergence of the notion and experience of an "open future," cf. Koyre 1957; Adam 1995; Adam and Groves 2007.

15. I have slighted the importance of the historicism and cultural relativism exemplified by the French *Encyclopédie* and by Giambattista Vico's *New Science*. Significantly, this assumption that new experiences are incorporated into existing semantic webs, or that the transformation of historical concepts comes by way of social history, is revised by Blumenberg (1997, 2010); and see the expert summary by Palti (2010). On this form of historicism as Orientalism, cf. Anidjar (2006, 68), who underscores Edward Said's point that the terms of secular science (race, character, type, origin) displaced the distinction between Christians and others. Anidjar indicates, via Said, how interpretations such as Koselleck's uncritically accept the notion that Orientalist practice arose through sudden access to knowledge about other places and forms. Evidently, Koselleck didn't go the whole length of his conclusion, given that he shares Said's concern with the transposition of Christian terms into what came to be figured as secular forms of knowledge.

16. See clarification and examples in, for example, Koselleck 2002, chapter 6. And read Blumenberg (2010), who argues against the notion that concepts necessarily emerge out of metaphor and for the position that linguistic metaphor imparts experience.

17. This is an extremely condensed presentation of Koselleck's analysis, the main points of which can be found in 2002, chapters 10 and 13; 2004; and 2006, 370–71. He notes the contrast with prior historical experience: "Historical experience therefore related itself to the present, a present which in its forward movement collected the past without, however, being able to significantly change itself *Nil novum sub sole*: this was true both for classical antiquity and for Christians awaiting the Last Judgment" (2004, 133).

18. Koselleck's writings offer a similar account of the concept of progress, arguing that by the nineteenth century the concept of progress no longer entails a figurative, spatial referent; and demonstrating how, since Kant, it has served to synthesize a manifold of scientific and social meanings (2002, 218–35).

19. Kathleen Davis objects to Koselleck's use of "modernity" as a category of explanation and as a self-constituting, "sovereign" period. In contrast, she argues, "it is precisely the myth of this 'awakening' and the suppressed *writing* of a feudal past that continues to privilege a linear narrative of civil society, which both brackets slavery and preserves a European universal 'spirit of the law'" (2008, 26). Her work critiques Koselleck's manner of periodizing historical time on the basis of "the apprehension of historical time itself, taking as its ground an evacuated 'Middle Ages'" (15). She rightly notes: "His

theory of periodization may be persuasive when viewed from within the self-defining 'modern European' political discourse in which he is situated, and indeed it has accrued many advocates. But it cannot be separated from the contemporaneous and interrelated discourses of anthropology and Oriental-ism, which defined Europe's others in precisely the terms Koselleck applies to the Middle Ages, and which in effect it extends" (90). The discourses of anthropology and Orientalism are therefore "the context in which we should consider mid-twentieth-century efforts to buttress a divide between modern historical consciousness and a theologically entrapped Middle Ages incapable of history, and to disavow the intellectual basis of its own thinking about his-tory, temporality, and periodization" (2008, 15–16). Davis likewise insists that "theories of periodization and temporality in 'the Middle Ages' were more numerous, complex, and embattled than medieval/modern periodization, partly because hegemony was less consolidated, but also, of course, because 'the Middle Ages' is not a temporal or a geographical unity" (16). Her project dovetails with my own insofar as we share the concern for, as she puts it, "pos-sibilities inherent in resisting or *suspending* periodization" (16, emphasis in original) as well as the aim to show how certain historical concepts are not inherently temporal concepts.

20. We could digress and compare Löwith, for example, who rejects the claim of modern historical consciousness as emerging out of a break in the manner of conceptualizing history. In the opening of his *Meaning in History*, he says: "Against this common opinion that proper historical thinking begins only in modern times, with the eighteenth century, the following outline aims to show that philosophy of history originates with the Hebrew and Christian faith in a fulfillment and that it ends with the secularization of its eschatologi-cal pattern" (1949, 1–2). Löwith takes issue with the primacy of the Christian concept of a break with the law, and yet does not see "crisis" as part of that thematization (see, for instance, the opening line to his chapter on Vico: "The great crisis in the history of our understanding of history occurred . . ."). The import of doing so is highlighted by Davis's critique of the secularization nar-rative (2008). See note 25. And for refutation of Koselleck's account of secu-larization in terms of transposed eschatology, see Blumenberg [1966] 1983.

21. Read also Jameson 2002 on periodization and the problem of representing "radical structural change."

22. Translated elsewhere in Koselleck (2004, 38) as "World history is the world's tribunal." Taken from Schiller's poem "Resignation," first published in his journal *Thalia* in 1786, this usage of the term "world-history" was to have great effect, having been used by Schiller in his inaugural lecture to the chair of history at Jena in 1789, and then by Kant in his *Idea for a Universal World History* in 1784, and by Hegel as published in the *Jena Realphilosophie* in 1805–6. Cf. H. B. Acton's Introduction (1975) to Hegel's *Natural Law*.

23. Some counter Koselleck's portrayal of this intellectual history, noting that history has not been posited consistently as a site of redemption, but equally has been figured as a state of war, in which "true historical events" are rare. The question I pursue herein can be put to both Koselleck and those, like Rousseau, who hold this latter view: "What is the status of 'true' historical events?" I thank Jay Bernstein for urging me to consider the status of this alternative intellectual history.

24. Originally Koselleck's PhD dissertation, *Kritik und Krise: Eine Studie zur Pathogenese der bürgerlichen Welt* was published in 1959. Read also Koselleck [1979] 2004, which, by positing "modernity" as a qualitatively new historical consciousness, amounts to a revised position. Koselleck's overall project is Hegelian, but is best taken as theory and not a philosophy of history.

25. This insight is most often associated with Kant, Baudelaire, Benjamin, or Foucault. Cf. M. Foucault (1997a, 1997b) on Kant's notion of "becoming mature." Read also Edwards's lively commentary (2006) on *Critique and Crisis*, which illustrates the affinities between Koselleck and Foucault with regard to this modern (Enlightenment) attitude. Edwards highlights the problem of assuming the unity of "the Enlightenment," which obscures the heterogeneous dispositions that prevailed in seventeenth-century European intellectual and literary circles—a problem noted by Koselleck (1988, 3) in his preface to the English edition. In a comment on Foucault's lecture "What Is Critique?" Talal Asad (2008) raises a question that could be put to Koselleck as well: "It is not clear whether Foucault wishes us to understand that 'the critical attitude' is a characteristic only of the modern West, or that 'the critical attitude' distinctive of the modern West is quite different from what is found elsewhere—an attitude that enables it to think for the first time of 'the transcendent' in a way that permits humanity to make its own future." For an analysis of the operation of "modern" in Asad 2003, see Davis 2008, 11–15.

26. Habermas published his *habilitation* in 1962, the English translation appearing in 1989. On Koselleck's and Habermas's respective theses, cf. La Volpa 1992.

27. Lilla (2007) follows, in positivistic manner, classical work in moral philosophy and political theory to define "The Crisis"—the title of the opening chapter of his book—as the "great separation" between temporal and spiritual authority, or between politics (the state) and moral law (conscience). He appraises the emergence of the requirement for a separation between "speculation about the divine" and "scientific observation of human behavior," an account that is relevant to the genealogy of crisis. The question remains: did the separation actually obtain?

28. Much scrutiny has been given to the matter of the status of the sacred in Western historiography and to the status of the account of the achievement of secularized time. The lengthy bibliography includes Schmitt [1922] 1985;

Löwith 1949; Blumenberg [1966] 1983; Benjamin 1968; Said 1979; Osborne 1995; Bhargava 1998; Chakrabarty 2000; Asad 2003; Mufti 2004; Masuzawa 2005; Anidjar 2006; Bilgrami 2006; de Vries and Sullivan 2006; Davis 2008. Departing from Gil Anidjar's adroit statement, "secularism is a name Christianity gave itself when it invented religion, when it named its other or others as religions" (2006, 62), Kathleen Davis sheds light on "the double process by which Europe simultaneously narrated its own secularization and mapped regions elsewhere in the world according to newly consolidated conceptions of 'religion' and religious heritage" (2008, 77). Her thesis challenges Koselleck's methodology and conclusions and is a correlate to the project I present herein. In brief sum: "the liberation of Europe's political, economic, and social life from ecclesiastical authority and religion was defined as the very basis of politics, progress, and historical consciousness; correlatively, Europe's 'medieval' past and cultural others, mainly colonized non-Christians, were defined as religious, static and ahistorical—thus open for narrative and territorial development" (77). Her inquiry into the practice of periodization illustrates how the emergence of the very concepts of feudalism and secularization gave rise to "the Middle Ages as a period concept." She illustrates how the notion of a "feudal" past for Europe was the product of juridical debates regarding the grounds and legitimacy of sovereignty, and thus argues: "'secular modernity' as a self-constituting sovereign period exposes the degree to which claims to sovereignty found themselves upon periodization" (78). Ultimately, Davis suggests that "critical analysis continues to struggle with its temporal legacy" (77)—a point of convergence with my own project on the concept of crisis.

29. See Gourevitch 1998, viii. Koselleck narrates the "other side of the Enlightenment": claims to a new society articulated by the Illuminati were made in the name of political impotence and concealed aspirations to power. This "secret" of the Masonic lodges is perhaps the underbelly of Habermas's depiction of the role of public rational discourse in social change. The Republic of Letters and the Masonic lodges took on political functions despite claims to a nonpolitical sphere of morality, their assertion of political legitimacy being foremost an assertion of moral innocence.

30. Loewenstein (1976), Carr (1987), Edwards (2006), and Davis (2008), among others, raise these questions. Edwards (2006) reviews and strongly counters the point that Koselleck's conceptual history is a teleological understanding of historical development, defined in terms of a series of semantic frames that culminate in a particular form of historical self-consciousness.

31. Loewenstein (1976, 122) further notes that Koselleck "uses" historical figures (e.g., Hobbes as an example of absolutist rationality) in a reductive mode of interpretation. However, my purpose is to indicate how Koselleck depicts the emergence of political utopianism through the seventeenth and eighteenth centuries. *Critique and Crisis* is a study of the historical conditions for the

subordination of politics to utopian ideology and is ultimately aimed at a better understanding of the conditions for German national socialism as well as the justification of war in the service of ideology, as in the case of both communism and liberalism during the Cold War. That Koselleck assumes an "existentialist-decisionist" form of politics (Loewenstein 1976, 123) is a point well taken, though not directly relevant to my commentary.

32. This "triumphalist history of the secular" (Asad 2003, 25), noted above, is not the main object of this essay. See notes 19, 28, 33, and 40 to this chapter for commentary.

33. Davis (2008, 94) puts this point succinctly in her work on feudalism and sovereignty: "Medievalists have long since tired of such attributions of stasis, closure, and homogeneity, so distortive that they nearly defy response. But response on an empirical basis would in any case be beside the point, for the problem that engages Koselleck as well as his predecessors and successors on this topic is not at all empirical, despite frequent recourse to empirical evidence. It is a philosophical struggle concerning the radical newness—or the possibility of radical newness—of *Neuzeit*, and its arguments, as well as its relevance for us today, turn on the structure of sovereignty and its relation to theology." This attention to philosophical categories in the practice of conceptual history has been noted with regard to Schmitt, Löwith, and their peers. The unending debates that have ensued between Schmitt, Koselleck, Löwith, and Blumenberg, as well as among contemporary scholars regarding secularization theses and whether or not one can denote a qualitative difference, marked as "modernity" or "*Neuzeit*" can be reviewed elsewhere.

34. To clarify Koselleck's point about Hobbes: "The development of reason is one of man's tasks, and though it grows out of instinctual nature, it can be achieved only through the regulation of a sensual and affective nature. It can further be helped by a rational education at the universities . . . or by a monarch using his jurisdiction in an enlightened manner to educate man. But this task of man for progress based on reason is not, however, determined by rational history but by the State" (Koselleck, 1988, 34, fn 37).

35. Cf. *De Cive* published in 1642, *Leviathan* published in 1651, and *Behemoth* published in 1682 on the tails of many prior pirated publications (see Mastnak 2009). The ample primary and secondary sources on Hobbes's writing and on the debates reviewed by Koselleck cannot be referenced herein. For a set of recent and very relevant essays, cf. Creppell, Lund, Mastnak, and especially Springborg, all in Mastnak 2009.

36. While peace might be desired as the highest good, its guarantee requires the obligation to forge artificial bonds to the Leviathan, making the highest *moral* good eminently *political* in character. While Hobbes ostensibly does away with the distinction between morality and politics in this way, he nevertheless displaces it to the extra-theological realm: the distinction between good and evil

in Christian moral philosophy is displaced to an extra-theological discursive domain in terms of war versus peace (Koselleck 1988, 24–25). To explore this gross summary of Koselleck's argument, read Koselleck 1988, chapter 2.

37. The claim is not that Hobbes formulated the idea of "private conscience" or "moral conscience." In trying to keep my sites on "crisis" and Koselleck, I cannot do justice to the myriad debates in both theology and what we now call political theory that transpired on this theme. Locke, Spinoza, and Rousseau wrote formidable texts; see most especially Rousseau's strange and beautiful *Emile*.

38. One could of course contest this linear reading of change from Hobbes to Locke, but my aim is to present Koselleck's argument concerning their work.

39. See, for example, Locke's *Essay Concerning Human Understanding*, book 2.

40. A point made by Talal Asad (2008) in his comment on *Critique and Crisis*: "The use of critique here turned out to be as much an argument for the necessity of faith as it was an attack on the absolute reliability of reason." Cf. "Is Critique Secular? Historical Notes on the Idea of Secular Criticism," posted on The Immanent Frame (ssrc blog), January 25, 2008, accessed November 17, 2008, http://www.ssrc.org/blogs/immanent_frame/.

41. While agreeing that this challenge was generalized extensively from an epistemological point of view, one nevertheless might wonder whether this positing of a transcendent and the consequential challenge of redemption, or negation of alienation, are truly general to world populations. See note 40.

42. See Davis 2008 for refutation of Koselleck's figuration of "premodern" consciousness. Again, my intention is not to underscore the empirical accuracy of his work; I am rather concerned with the historiography of the term "crisis" and its consequential practice.

43. The notion of progress implied by Leibniz's metaphysics is crucial to the performance of human history in terms of the goal of the just organization of society. Both Rousseau and Kant are singular references for Koselleck of the position that human morality must be adapted to knowledge. Koselleck's analysis of the historical concept of "progress" clarifies the points made herein (cf. notably 2002, chapter 8). Here one could also note Husserl's position that modern science is an aberrant development of modern reason, which inspires his question of how this crisis in reason came about. Cf. Luhmann 2002 and Dodd 2004, chapter 1.

44. Critchley (2007, 16–17) gives a list of the various contents of this formal demand:

> Mosaic Law in the Bible, the Good beyond Being in Plato, the resurrected Christ in Paul and Augustine, the Good as the goal of desire for Aquinas, the practical ideal of generosity for Descartes, the experience of benevolence for Hutcheson, and of sympathy for Adam Smith and Hume, the greatest happiness of the greatest number for Bentham and Mill,

the moral law in Kant, practical faith as the goal of subjective striving in Fichte, the abyssal intuition of freedom in Schelling, the creature's feeling of absolute dependency on the creator in Schleiermacher, pity for the suffering of one's fellow human beings in Rousseau or for all creatures in Schopenhauer, the thought of eternal return in Nietzsche, the ethico-teleological idea of the Kantian sense in Husserl, the call of conscience in Heidegger, the relation to the Thou in Buber, the claim of the non-identical in Adorno, etc. etc.

He proposes a model of ethical experience in terms of the affirmation of such a demand. See also Critchley 2001 on Badiou and *l'événement*.

45. It is important to underscore that Koselleck interrogates the concept as historically produced and hence contingent, but nevertheless argues for the necessity of the concept of crisis.

46. See also Furet 1978 [English edition, 1981]. Edwards (2006, 440) calls attention to Furet's influential reinterpretation of the French Revolution, where he distinguishes between the utopianism inherent in revolt, as a return to an idealized past, and the utopian future inherent to revolution, which necessitates a break with the past. Note also that Koselleck does not infer that revolutionary practice thus subverts what he defines as the structure of modernity; rather, it is enabled by it, and serves to extend its premises, a point also made by Niklas Luhmann.

47. Koselleck's point, reiterated by Wellmer (1993) and Rasch (2000), is that revolutionary praxis, being enabled by what he sees as the structure of modernity, only serves to confirm or extend modernity, not negate or surpass it.

48. Cf. Koselleck 1988, 117–23, and the remarks in Gourevitch's preface (viii–ix).

49. The implications of this metaphysics of time are pursued in Osborne 1995. Inspired by Koselleck's characterization of modernity as a specific, paradoxical form of temporality, Osborne reflects on the extent to which the ontological status of historical time could be understood independently of theological connotations. My reflections on crisis are relevant to his examination of our pursuit of what he calls the "ontological structure of historical time."

50. For commentary on this interrogation, cf. H. White's foreword to Koselleck 2002, viii–xiv.

51. Hayden White's annotation (1973, 37–38) is worth noting: "In Irony, figurative language folds back on itself and brings its own potentialities for distorting perception under question. . . . [It appears] to signal the ascent of thought in a given area of inquiry to a level of self-consciousness on which a genuinely 'enlightened'—that is to say, self-critical—conceptualization of the world and its processes has become possible. . . . It is, in short, a model of the linguistic protocol in which skepticism in thought and relativism in ethics are conveniently expressed."

52. Among many examples, cf. Schmitt's parody of progress, "Die Buribunken"

(1918); but already in the mid-eighteenth century, Voltaire had penned *Candide* ([1759] 1969).

53. Browne (2008, 7) puts this point succinctly: "Critical theory seeks to identify the potentials for emancipation immanent in the needs of subjects and aims to provide an analysis of contemporary society that apprehends its developmental possibilities."

54. In that sense, he takes reason to be procedural, or a form of "communicative rationality."

55. Butler asks (2002, 212): "What is it to offer a critique?" Her aim, via Foucault's original text, is to differentiate between "a critique of this or that position and critique as a more generalized practice," which leads her to ask some crucial questions: "Can we even ask such a question about the generalized character of critique without gesturing toward an essence of critique? And if we achieved the generalized picture, offering something which approaches a philosophy of critique, would we then lose the very distinction between philosophy and critique that operates as part of the definition of critique itself?"

56. Foucault's essay, a preliminary reflection on the complementary and equally tenacious question, "What Is Enlightenment?," was first published in the *Bulletin de la Société française de la philosophie* in 1990; for the English version, cf. Foucault 1997a. "Que'est-ce que les Lumières?" was first published in *Dits et Écrits* in 1994; for the English version, cf. Foucault 1997b. Though Butler comments only on the first text, I refer to both of his texts herein.

57. See Butler 2002 and Browne 2008, 7, for explanation. Butler notes that Foucault's break with the Enlightenment is found in his critical history, or his concern for what is "unthought" within its own terms, as well as his abandonment of reason as rational evaluation in favor of the question of what criteria specify the sorts of reasons that come to bear on subject formation. The enduring problem of reason is stated as follows: "But how do we move from understanding the reasons we might have for consenting to a demand to forming those reasons for ourselves in the course of producing those reasons (and, finally, putting at risk the field of reason itself)?" (2002, 218).

58. My guess is that this is true of authorship in general, though I cannot have pretense to have considered this issue beyond the realm of social science writing. One merely has to open a random series of fiction and nonfiction books to discover the numerous first chapters entitled "The Crisis."

59. A non-Foucauldian approach that similarly (and productively) inquires into the limits of intelligibility and the self-reflexive liberation of subjects as a prime mover in history is the sociology of critique. Cf. Boltanski and Thévenot 1991.

60. Jay Bernstein, personal communication, New York, February 3, 2010. Here one might pursue Deleuze's statement (1994, 227) that philosophy takes

place in paradox: "Paradox is the pathos or the passion of philosophy"—which applies to the social sciences more generally.

61. This problem of meaning is of course not simple and should not be taken as "what things, in themselves, mean." It is a problem that has been posed in existential terms, most notably by Husserl ([1954] 1970), who lamented that science had lost meaning for life. For Husserl, the universalization of formal logic led to the alienation of the idea of universal philosophy from the accomplishment of its method: "Ultimately, all modern sciences drifted into a peculiar, increasingly puzzling crisis with regard to the meaning of their original founding as branches of philosophy, a meaning which they continued to bear within themselves" (12). This problem of what is "meaningful" leads Husserl to conclude, as James Dodd notes, that there is "a deeper life-crisis of European humanity, one that has led to the uninhabitability of the world not because there is something that cannot be understood, but because in objectivism, understanding itself [. . .] has lost its footing, giving rise to an existential crisis about the possibility of the very decision it represents for human existence—the decision about what is to count as meaningful and meaningless" (2004, 39). The crisis or failure is not, for Husserl, "scientific thinking"; rather, its very success resulted in its failure, external to its project, for human existence (see especially Husserl [1954] 1970, 52–53).

62. As I noted in the introduction (note 15), the mere act of posing these questions is a form of critique. I am not "against" this practice of critique; but I am noting how it posits crisis as an a priori and how the very grounds for knowledge of such crisis are not elaborated. As we will see in chapter 3 below, I am likewise reiterating the point that "critique has run out of steam," as envisaged by Latour 2004.

63. This is not a novel or necessarily remarkable point. It is reviewed with clarity by William Rasch (2000 and 2002), and see Knodt (1994) on paradox and self-reference in Habermas and Luhmann.

64. There are many classes of paradox, one of which is the antinomies. Cf. Quine 1966, 1–21. I thank Richard Bernstein for his conversation with me about the antinomies.

65. This point can be pursued relative to the question of history and historical error, posed herein, in Rockmore and Margolis 2006. But read Bernstein (1983, 2010) on incommensurability.

66. I have grossly simplified the point for expediency. Referring to it herein indicates how this thought-piece on crisis serves a history of reason. Put succinctly by Angelica Nuzzo: "The thesis that allows both Kant and Hegel to insert . . . the condition of history at the very heart of scientific rationality regards not directly the idea of truth, but rather, respectively, the possibility of *error* in our quest for truth" (2006, 79, emphasis in original). Deleuze and

Guattari (1996) state this differently: because the form of time as becoming brings truth into crisis, falsity governs narration—perhaps an iteration of my insistence on the foundational question, what went wrong? See also Rasch in Luhmann 2002, 6–7.

67. Not able to read German, I content myself with Rasch's helpful presentation of Fuchs's work in English. The ultimate reference for Rasch is Niklas Luhmann.

68. This excerpt is from one of Luhmann's rare explanations of his relationship to constructivism published in English. It is quoted in Christis 2001, which I rely on heavily for his clear presentation and his translation of Luhmann's accompanying German-language texts.

69. Christis's lucid presentation of Luhmann's theory of knowledge clarifies Luhmann's opposition to metaphysical realism, presenting the sense in which his work can be characterized as realist, as well as the senses in which his approach does not partake of idealism, skepticism, or radical constructivism. Rabinow (2008, 62–63) sums this up well: "Luhmann's entire work is at pains to show that the founding distinction of a system is, by definition, arbitrary—in the mathematical sense of the term. This does not mean it is false, but only that once a distinction is drawn it carries with it exclusions and blind spots. . . . Once one sees and accepts this basic requirement of arbitrariness as a condition of analytical rigor, then systems theory can move in good faith from that arbitrariness to a kind of realism. Luhmann can proceed to give us an epochal description of modernity as contingency, knowing full well that it is arbitrary."

70. See Luhmann's German texts: *Erkenntnis als Konstruktion* (1988) and *Die Wissenschaft der Gesellschaft* (1990). Christis clarifies (2001, 335): "In a first step, Luhmann proposes to start from the distinction between system and environment, a distinction that replaces both the ontological one between being and non-being and the epistemological one between subject and object. The epistemic subject or knowing person is now replaced by the observing biological, psychic or social system. To avoid misunderstandings: Luhmann does not deny the existence of persons. But first, persons are not systems, and second, if we want to know what the concept of person means, we have to look at the social system in which this concept is used."

71. Luhmann's abstract concept of observation does not require an observer or a method of observation: because he takes "the social" to be a system of communication, observation denotes the distinction that is realized in the simultaneous apprehension of two sides, such as exterior and interior, or inside and outside: "Distinguishing what is different makes sense only when positing an underlying identity that permits realizing what is different" (Luhmann 1990b, 130). For Luhmann, "society" is not an a priori domain; it is best construed as a cybernetic system.

72. This brief allusion to observing systems can be explored in Luhmann's immense body of work, in part inspired by George Spencer-Brown. For clarification, see Rasch 2000; Moeller 2006; and Arnoldi 2001.

73. Although Luhmann does not assess the term "crisis" in this manner, his appraisal of Husserl's *The Crisis of European Sciences and Transcendental Phenomenology* [1954] (1970) can be read through such a lens, as I have done (see Luhmann 2002, chapter 1). Luhmann makes reference to the emergence of historical time à la Koselleck and the concomitant emphasis on salvation. He remarks (41): "If one poses the question of what remains unilluminated or excluded when one proclaims self-critical reason as the historical heritage and obligation of 'European humanity,' one ends with the question of whether (and how) this, too, may be recovered once more in self-critical reflection. That could be indeed. But if so, then it would demand entirely different theoretical figures than those that are held in readiness in the concept of the transcendental subject, Husserl's paradigmatic figure." As I noted above, crisis is taken as shorthand for a crisis of epistemology or a crisis of subjectivity, per its usage by many scholars, from Husserl to Foucault. These evocations of crisis as a matter of epistemology are bound up in the "paradox of subjectivity"; they are symptomatic of the persistence of the philosophical problem of the transcendental subject. "The paradox of subjectivity" is an expression used by Husserl in *The Crisis of European Sciences*, and taken up most distinctly by David Carr (1999).

74. "There is no position outside of society from which to communicate, but a system can internally test semantic references which may be treated as absolute" (Luhmann 1990b, 133). "Inviolate level of order" is Luhmann's expression (133), taken from Hofstadter. With regard to distinctions that posit external reference points serving as standards for evaluation, Luhmann says (2002, 183): "Everyone knows, of course, that the word 'human being' is not a human being. We must also learn that there is nothing in the unity of an object that corresponds to the word. Words such as 'human being,' 'soul,' 'person,' 'subject,' and 'individual' are nothing more than what they effect in communication. They have limited connectability and therefore have a potential for distinction and definition." He clarifies (1990b, 107–43) how the distinction between individual and society posits an external reference point, an argument found in his writing generally (cf. 2002) and in his criticism of Habermas particularly (cf. Knodt 1994).

75. The most familiar example being the Socratic paradox: "I know that I know nothing at all." Rasch (2002, 19) restates this nicely, with reference to Patrick Grim (1991): "An omniscient mind, to be omniscient, would have to be minimally self-reflective, but since it can be demonstrated that no such self-reflective mind can be truly omniscient, there simply can be no omniscient mind. Even for God, the universe is 'incomplete.' God may know everything,

but God cannot know everything God knows." This problem of paradox was apprehended by German idealism as the problem of self-consciousness.

76. This brings me to the crux of my initial intrigue with the concept of crisis, my question being how to think "Africa" otherwise than under the sign of crisis— that is, otherwise than in terms of pathology. See Roitman (forthcoming).

77. This must be my performative paradox ("Crisis is . . ."). I follow Luhmann's definition: "The distinction that is operatively used in observation but not observable is the observer's blind spot" (2002, 190). Cf. Rasch's introductory remarks (2000, 104–5) on this notion of blind spot.

78. It is worth noting, as an aside, how Paul Rabinow's particular style of inquiry, or anthropology of the contemporary, responds to this dilemma:

> Such happenings [forms/events] are not reducible to the elements involved any more than they are representative of the epoch, its instantiation. Nor are such forms/events mysterious and unanalyzable although it is hard to do with the conceptual tools at hand. It is only that so much effort has been devoted in the name of social science to explaining away the emergence of new forms as the result of something else that we lack adequate means to conceptualize the forms/events as the curious and potent singularities that they are. To identify and analyze singularities, however, is by no means to deny their contemporary status and consequently their interconnections with many other things in the world. (1999, 180)

79. "The blind spot of each observation, the distinction it employs at the moment, is at the same time its guarantee of a world" (Luhmann 2002, 136).

2. CRISIS NARRATIVES

1. This could be taken as a straightforward constructivist position. But one should note: to refer to "all possible worlds" is not to refer to "any possible world." My point is not that worlds are wholly contingent and fundamentally constructed—that is, that even nature is not "natural" but social, or socially constructed. Instead, I take up the adage, "The More Constructed the More Real" (Latour 2003, 33). In response to the standard query—"Is constructed reality constructed or real?"—Latour laments the standard reply: both. As he explains,

> To prove that matters of facts have been "constructed," it is argued, one has simply to show that they are contingent, that they could have been otherwise, that they are not necessary. To disprove the constructivist account, it is counterargued, one has simply to show that there are no two ways for X to exist, only one. But such a debate is a profound misreading of the real argument in science studies, especially in the history of science. The point is not about demonstrating the existence of "alternative" physics, chemistry, or genetics, but about the impossibility of absorbing the world—in

the singular—in one single chunk. . . . Danger, contingency, uncertainty, does not qualify the result—which might well be Necessity herself—but the process through which "the" world becomes progressively shared as one *same* world. (39, emphasis in original)

For different views on the dilemma of the constructivist position, see also, among others, Rorty 1979; Bernstein 1983; Hacking 1999; Meillassoux 2008.

2. Tom Braithwaite's reference to the "canon of crisis analysis" appears in his commentary on the Financial Crisis Inquiry Commission's report, published in January 2001, which Braithwaite encapsulates as follows: "Twenty months, 700 interviews, 571 pages and the first official US government report into the causes of the financial crisis found that—as in the Murder on the Orient Express—everyone did it" (2011). Professor Andrew Lo of MIT reviews twenty-one scholarly and journalist accounts, only to conclude "we're left with several mutually inconsistent narratives, none of which completely satisfies our need for redemption and closure" (2012, 151).

3. This is not an exhaustive list; it is meant to provide a representative sampling of the literature and does not include the technical literature in the academic field of economics, to which some of these authors nonetheless refer. There is also a plethora of special issues of academic journals and popular media devoted to these themes.

4. Some theorists define crisis in terms of the problem of valuing liquidity in time as opposed to the value of underlying assets. Scholes (2009), for instance, raises this issue of liquidity prices, which he contrasts to underlying commodity prices, and locates as the central issue for intermediation and forecasting. Crisis, for Scholes, is produced by the breakdown in financial intermediation, which is a matter of inventory turnover that generates liquidity.

5. I am of course giving an extremely abbreviated version of their accounts; but the latter are well known and easily consulted. It is important to note that their analyses are concerned with both consumer credit and sovereign debt, which were financed on a global scale from East Asian sources.

6. And the extent of the recent credit expansion is of course not unique to contemporary narratives of financial or economic history: for accounts of various credit expansions, mostly depicted as cycles of recurring history, see Brenner 2002 and 2006 (Marxist-inspired); Cooper 2008 (neo-Keynesian); and Krippner 2011 (who combines the two approaches).

7. My schematic reductionism is meant to serve my illustration; it glosses the intricacies of the various arguments as well as the real differences of interpretation regarding subjects like inflation, wage stagnation, the role of the collapse of the Bretton Woods system, the role of the central bank or a clearing bank, et cetera.

8. I thank Martha Poon for sending me his review article.

9. The distinction between debt as a form of wealth and debt as a liability is pursued in Roitman 2005, chapter 4.

10. The mere act of posing these questions is a form of critique insofar as they are questions about how certain orderings of the world foreclose alternative accounts. In that sense, my practice of critique follows that of Michel Foucault, as presented above.

11. A subordinate question is: when do the mainstream media decide to print copy announcing, in extra-large font and in the boldest type, "**Crisis**," given that this very enunciation generates the proverbial bank run? A study of the editorial process, which gives rise to these rare and powerful statements, should be undertaken. For a rare foray, see Jacobs 1996.

12. This book won't provide comprehensive answers to those questions. My aim is to raise them so as to indicate what kinds of questions crisis narratives foreclose. On the topic of credit-debt and value, see Roitman 2003. On the question of how, during the 1980s and 1990s, debt came to be figured as an asset through the "high-leverage movement," involving specific financial models and managerial techniques, read Poon and Wosnitzer 2012. The anthropological work that has inspired my research on debt-value includes Appadurai 1986; Munn 1986; Parry and Bloch 1989; Thomas 1991; Strathern 1992; Weiner 1992; Gudeman 2001; Guyer 2004; Elyachar 2005; Maurer 2006b; and see Maurer's review (2006a) and Peebles's review (2010).

13. The risk of loss on a CDO portfolio is divided by financial analysts into "tranches," which have different priority rankings due to their variable risk/reward evaluation and in spite of a uniform collateral base. Smith (2010) reviews the creation of hybrid CDOs, which afford very high profit margins to originators, or those operating in the "shadow banking" system, by which she means institutional sites that were not fully regulated (see Mehrling 2011 and Pozsar et al. 2010; and not to be confused with deregulation per Riles 2011). Significantly, Mehrling characterizes the purchase of insurance to hedge risk in terms of valuation, arguing therefore against the notion that mortgage-backed securities were fictive forms of value.

14. For a similar approach to the emergence of organized financial-derivatives trading and LIBOR (London interbank offered rate), cf. MacKenzie 2007.

15. Riles's empirical research inquires into the use of contracts to set aside collateral in order to secure derivative products; her attention to private regulatory solutions in financial markets, and the legal or institutional practices that permit collateral relations, while slighted here, is clearly relevant, and is a point pursued below.

16. Yves Smith goes so far as to say that the "CDOs would not have existed without the shorts, and the trade continued because you had many actors making decisions based on trading games where the quality of the CDOs was

utterly irrelevant" (Naked Capitalism blog post, March 25, 2010, http://www .nakedcapitalism.com/, accessed March 26, 2010.

17. In January 2008, the CDS market alone was said to be worth approximately $45 trillion, which is, as Wolfgang Münchau (2008) says, "not an easy figure to imagine. It is more than three times the annual gross domestic product of the US."

18. Poon and Wosnitzer's review of Karen Ho's *Liquidated* asks an important question in that regard: "The question this book raises for us is this: can a uniform 'culture of Wall Street' (if such a thing exists) held in the minds and hearts of people working inside IBS [investment banks] be held responsible for the profound changes that have taken place in American corporate governance, changes which began not in the mid-1990s, but with the LBOS [leveraged buyouts] of the 1980s?" (2012, 250). This section of the book benefited enormously from conversations with Martha Poon and her many insightful edits. I likewise thank Robert Wosnitzer for confirming my intuitions about Lewis's account (personal communications, August 2011).

19. Although most studies grouped under the *économie des conventions*, sociology of accounting and economic calculation, and social studies of finance rubrics avoid the virtual/real or false value/true value distinctions, Maurer (2008) is an explicit statement about the effects of assuming these distinctions, which serve wrongheaded arguments for "resocializing" finance. See also Callon 1998; Beunza, Hardie, and MacKenzie 2006; MacKenzie 2006; MacKenzie, Muniesa, and Siu 2007; Çalişkan and Callon 2009. And see Miyazaki and Riles 2005 on the failure of economic knowledge as a form of efficacy—an endpoint, and not a deviation.

20. The anthropology of value is crucial to the study of these processes and practices of valuation. Taking cues and/or distance from Marx and Mauss, the anthropological tradition is represented most distinctly by Appadurai 1986; Hart 1986, 2000; Munn 1986; Strathern 1988, 1992; Guyer 1995, 2004; Keane 2001; Maurer 2003, 2005, 2006b; Elyachar 2005; Roitman 2005. Some research on property (Verdery 2003; Verdery and Humphrey 2004) and property rights (Hayden 2003) attends to practices of valuation. More recently, work in economic sociology and the social studies of finance has taken up the study of valuation, with attention to the constitutive and performative roles of calculative practices and technical infrastructures: for examples, see Miller and Napier 1993; Hopwood and Miller 1994; Miller 2008; Çalişkan and Callon 2009, 2010; Latour and Lépinay 2009; Çalişkan 2010; Beckert and Aspers 2011; and see Poon and Wosnitzer 2012 and the new journal *Valuation Studies*.

21. "Brick and mortar" is Martha Poon's fitting expression for houses and the housing market (personal communication, January 11, 2012).

22. Martha Poon cites a working paper published in 2004 by the Joint Center for Housing Studies at Harvard University, which indicates the priority placed on *pricing* default risk in subprime markets over the prime markets. This report analyzes the relationship between FICO scores and mortgage coupons (interest rates) using Standard and Poor's proprietary database. As Poon notes, the conclusion as to the rational pricing of risk in the non-GSE market is tautological in its reasoning, since the authors use FICO scores to show that the market is rational. Her research shows that it is "the rationale of FICO that has made the market able to perform this rationality" (2009, 668).

23. Different figures are given according to which aspects of the finance and credit markets are being assessed. Grossberg notes (2010, 298–99), without specifying the timing of the assessment, "The debt market was estimated to produce 4.8 percent of gross domestic product (GDP), but provided over 30 percent of corporate profits and 10 percent of wages." He also notes, with reference to a Bank for International Settlements report, that there were "$596 trillion of OTC (over the counter) derivatives as of December 7, and $344 trillion of derivatives sold on the various exchanges as of December 2005." Likewise, he reports, with reference to Bryan and Rafferty (2007) that "derivates added approximately $200 trillion to the global money supply, and there were approximately $2.5 trillion in derivatives transacted daily. Add to that $12 trillion in asset backed securities, plus $60 trillion in collateralized debt swaps (insuring $5 trillion in bonds)."

24. The point that the bubble-making bubblistas and the missed-bubble bubblistas seem to be one and the same is suggested by Clover, with much after-the-fact moralizing: "But this alibi was itself a bubble. As with the economy itself, once the alibi bubble burst, and the wishful thinking and corruption leaked out, the underlying facts began to present themselves. A couple, or several, okay really quite a few folks had called it. Robert Shiller of the Case-Shiller Home Price Index rose to the fore among them; he had called the dot-com bust as well. Nouriel Roubini, business professor and head of the consulting outfit Roubini Global Economics, achieved media ubiquity—his dire forecasts and dour demeanor would earn him the title of 'Dr. Doom.' Dean Baker, founder of the Center for Economic and Policy Research, had not only issued warnings, but in 2004 sold his home in a recently gentrified quarter of Washington, DC—the gentleman's way of betting against the market. Then there are the less gentlemanly sorts found in Michael Lewis's *The Big Short*, who made millions and billions by seeing it coming" (Clover 2011).

25. These forceful statements should be read alongside Barry, Osborne, and Rose 1996; Rose 1999; and Miller and Rose 2008.

26. This narrative line is the bread and butter of twentieth-century social science and need not be spelled out here. The epistemological grounds for these spaces of alleged autonomy are best excavated rather than assumed, as many

have pointed out: see Foucault 1970 on production of the boundaries of the disciplines: and see Callon 1998 and Maurer 2008 for replies to this desire for resocialization of the economy.

27. The crisis of neoliberalism is put forth by Harvey 2005; Calhoun and Derluguian 2011; Duménil and Lévy 2011; and assumed by countless others.

28. The indeterminacy of neoliberalism, as a category, has been noted by some scholars, who seek to understand the specific laws, policies, or technical mechanisms of neoliberal governing: cf. Brenner and Theodore 2002; Hartman 2005; Somers 2005, 2008; Mudge 2008; Chorev 2010; Collier 2011; Riles 2011. And read Barry, Osborne, and Rose 1996; Rose 1999; and Elyachar 2012.

29. See also Arrighi 1994; Jessop 2000, 2002; and Harvey 2011; though noting that, contrary to Arrighi, Jessop, and Harvey, Krippner (2011) does not maintain that contemporary financialization represents a discrete or novel phase of capitalist development.

30. Krippner's account replaces the "deregulation then crisis" narrative with "crisis then deregulation," a point of commentary below.

31. The social science disciplines of anthropology and sociology are particularly devoted to this view; the bibliography is extensive. For a recent statement from cultural studies, cf. Hayward 2010, 284 and the contributions to Hayward 2010 and Hay 2010.

32. This position disregards other studies of derivatives. On the emergence of the very demand for derivatives as forms of knowledge, or the techniques (probabilistic concepts, stochastic modeling) that have generated derivatives as virtual practice (i.e., something that can be acted upon, and hence is not false, unreal or "impossible") cf. Arnoldi 2004. On financial derivatives and the *material* production of "virtuality," or the requirement of facticity for measure, cf. MacKenzie 2007. On the equity derivatives business as a site of financial engineering and innovation, cf. Lépinay 2011.

33. Grossberg claims that the contemporary crisis is both a "crisis of modernity" and a crisis of "multiple modernities." He explains (2010, 311): "We are beginning to see the possibility that the contemporary crisis is only a part of the ongoing story of the multiple and fragmented struggles with, within and against a way of living . . . constituting what I call a way of being modern that found its fullest expression in the post-war Western capitalist democracies. I have called this 'liberal modernity.'" He notes (313) that it is important to avoid potentially reinscribing a logic of the very modernity that he seeks to challenge, and so hopes to "decolonize the practices of conjunctural analysis." Positing "multiple modernities" might also reinscribe such logics.

34. Langley characterizes his work as a "cultural economy" approach, referring to Pryke and du Gay (2007). I owe thanks to Bill Maurer for directing me to Langley's work.

35. Personal communication, March 25, 2012.

36. Langley takes this expression from MacKenzie (2004) and his notion of "counterperformativity."

37. It is central to the respective oeuvres of Gilles Deleuze, Félix Guattari, Richard Bernstein, Bruno Latour, Quentin Meillassoux, among many others. And the pragmatics of valuation has been central to the research of scholars such as Jane Guyer, Marilyn Strathern, Nigel Thrift, Michel Callon, Fabien Muniesa, and Bill Maurer.

38. This point, not elaborated extensively herein, is the subject of Roitman forthcoming.

39. The obvious reference to this thesis is Walter Benjamin, though a contemporary view of capitalism as permanent crisis is put forth by Hardt and Negri 2000. In response, see the helpful commentary by Peter Osborne on the recent (and, he feels, predictable) revival of interest in Marxist crisis theory, which gestures toward my apparently eccentric assertion that crisis never obtains. He states that "crisis is constituted as a historical category according to a structure of thought within which it is speculatively political (that is, it has a political meaning) but is nonetheless, in any particular instance, *politically irresolvable* (that is, is not amenable to political action). The historical concept of crisis thus registers *an aporia in the historical concept of politics*. In other words, what I earlier called 'the crisis of Marxist political thought' runs far deeper than Marx's work, down to the bedrock of all philosophico-historical concepts of political practice" (2010, 22–23, emphasis in original). This view, as he notes, extends Koselleck's account of the emergence of the concept of "history" as a utopian philosophical concept. I thank Ann Stoler for bringing Osborne's article to my attention, twice.

40. By "anthropological insights" I refer to a general anthropology that is not limited to the practice of ethnography or the discipline of anthropology. Vigh claims (2008, 15), "The interesting thing about the perspective of 'crisis as context' is that it leads us to realize that new configurations are sought [and] established, even in situations where social instability and volatility prevail, and that it grants us an analytical optic able to engage anthropologically in such social processes." See also Ortiz 2011, who notes that "anthropology is already a gesture of crisis." This approach is basic to contemporary social science practice; for a few examples, see Boltanski and Thévenot 1991; Greenhouse, Mertz, and Warren 2002; Hoffman and Oliver-Smith 2002; Roitman 2005; and Vigh 2008.

41. Personal communication, Kartikeya Saboo, who participated in meetings of these groups for preliminary doctoral research.

42. Ortiz (2011) confirms this point: "If crisis there is, it has not touched the financial imagination that frames the practices of financial professionals, defines their procedures and legitimate controversies within them."

43. This slogan originated on a Tumblr blog launched in August 2011 by a young New York activist. In May 2011, Joseph Stiglitz had referred to the extreme income gap between the richest and poorest Americans in a *Vanity Fair* article entitled "Of the 1%, by the 1%, for the 1%." Brian Stelter, "Camps Are Cleared but '99 Percent' Still Occupies the Lexicon," *New York Times*, November 30, 2001, accessed January 8, 2012, http://www.nytimes.com/2011/12/01/us/we -are-the-99-percent-joins-the-cultural-and-political-lexicon.html?_r=1&scp. However, the anthropologist David Graeber is often attributed with coining the expression "We Are the 99%" in his article "Occupy Wall Street Rediscovers the Radical Imagination," appearing in the *Guardian*, September 25, 2011.

44. Shank (2008) makes a similar observation with regard to Theodore Rabb's classic *The Struggle for Stability in Early Modern Europe* (1975), noting that the term "crisis" is "a metaphor and analytical-narrative device that works to show similarities between a range of different yet synchronous areas." Thanks to Orit Halpern for sending me Shank's review.

45. That is, also unexamined are the ways that acts of witnessing and testimony are figured as the means by which victims relocate themselves as survivors (see LaCapra 2004, 175–76). Some insist upon witnessing and narration as a moral imperative to not forget. My point is not to recommend an ethics of forgetting and oblivion. My aim is to note how crisis is a non-locus for narration, which permits the constitution of "trauma" as a historical category. Such narration is not "bad"; it requires epistemological self-reflexivity. I thank Jay Bernstein for urging me to clarify this point.

46. One of the most obvious practices of this ethics of bearing witness is contemporary humanitarianism. For elaboration, see Redfield (2005, 2006, 2010), who explores how states of crisis found an ethics of action for humanitarian practice, with reference to Doctors without Borders. Without attention to the ways in which the imperative to bear witness is a historically Christian ethical imperative that entails the judgment of history per se, Redfield's inquiry into how crisis constitutes humanitarianism does not consider how humanitarianism has become a late twentieth-century form of social and political critique, a striking—almost uncanny—manifestation of the mutual constitution of critique and crisis documented by Koselleck. Recall Koselleck's point that claims to a moral imperative mark out a pre-political sphere, denoting the separation between morality (conscience) and politics (the state), or the notion of a private inner space as the natural site for social critique—what Koselleck ([1959] 1988) called the "apolitical politics." Without theological justification for human suffering, this form of witnessing seeks to inscribe human drama in a form of secular, historical narrative. Redfield demonstrates that there are ongoing discussions about the appropriate ways and means of witnessing within the organization, but the *very possibility of representation itself* is left unquestioned. For commentary, cf. Roitman forthcoming.

47. For LaCapra, this presupposition of crisis is to be contrasted to an anthropo-logical or historical approach "that does not begin with, or become fixated on, breakdown or aporia but is open and alert to such breakdown or aporia when it occurs in the witness's attempt to recount traumatic experience" (2004, 174).

48. Although not a book on "crisis," Jameson's *A Singular Modernity* (2002), a formal, narrative analysis of a seemingly nonnarrative category, makes this point with respect to the foundational ruptures that found modernity. J. B. Shank takes note of this: "Jameson ultimately comes to question the material and ontological reality of the decisive ruptures and breaks that modernist so-cial science makes foundational to developmental stories of historical change. The 'general crisis' framework is one such decisive moment of modernity-making change, and since for Jameson 'modernity is not a concept, philo-sophical or otherwise, but a narrative category,' his work invites us to rethink modern historical development through an invitation to critically scrutinize our categories of historical narration" (2008, 1097). See also Löwith 1949 and Davis 2008.

3. CRISIS: REFRAIN!

1. The bibliography is too extensive for full referencing; cf. the most widely cited works by Giddens 1991, 1999, 2003; Beck 1992, 1999, 2008. Beck (1992) characterizes "risk society" as having emerged from an epochal shift from industrial arrangements and attendant actuarial norms and practices to an "uninsured society," in which the relationship between the future and the present is compromised by a lack of linear narrativity (progress), guarantees for progress (technology), and the rise of a short-term calculus ("mathemati-cal ethics"). But see Luhmann 1993.

2. "Systemic Risk in Consumer Finance," *Limn*, no. 1, accessed July 2011, http://limn.it/systemic-risk-in-consumer-finance/.

3. A popular play-by-play account can be found in Sorkin's terribly hefty *Too Big to Fail* (2009), though with more intrigue and less analysis than other ac-counts.

4. Cooper (2008, 101–5) reviews the role of the coupling of mark-to-market ac-counting with debt-financed asset markets to account for these cycles. He likewise presents (chapter 3) a history of the rise of fiat money and CODs; the emergence of the contemporary form of debt markets; and the ways that the monetary system is secured via debt, noting that this was equally true under the gold standard. Permanent instability results, as for neo-Marxist accounts, from increases in the money supply, which entail increased debt.

5. Read Hacking 1975, 1990; Porter 1986; Daston 1988.

6. This presentation of views on systemic risk forgoes yet another discussion

of quantitative risk management and the attempt to eliminate so-called Knightian uncertainty, which can be found in publications in economic theory, finance, and social studies of finance. For a history of risk management, cf. Bernstein 1996a and 1996b; and see Hacking 2003. For discussion of the distinction between radical uncertainty and risk as intrinsic to the formalization of risk modeling and commentary on the impossibility of the distinction itself, see, for example, Starr, Rudman, and Whipple 1976; Porter 1995; Reddy 1996; and Power 2007; Cooper 2008, chapter 7; Skidelsky 2009. For a genealogical view, read Daston 1988; for a novel view of contemporary practice, read Millo and MacKenzie 2007 and Poon 2012; and for an alternative stance regarding the practice of apprehending contingency in terms of probability, read Ayache 2010.

7. See note 6 regarding Knightian uncertainty. From Power's perspective (2007, 26), "Much of what we today call risk management is 'uncertainty management' in Knightean terms." The emergence of the practice of risk management is widely commented in academic publications: see, among many others, Knights and Vurdubakis 1993; Bernstein 1996a, 1996b; Hacking 2003; O'Malley 2004.

8. In Luhmann's words (1993, 6): "If only for epistemological reasons, we may not assume that such a thing as risk exists, and that it is only a matter of discovering and investigating it. The conceptual approach constitutes what is being dealt with. The outside world itself knows no risks, for it knows neither distinctions, nor expectations, nor evaluations, nor probabilities—unless self-produced by observers systems in the environment of other systems." Jac Christis elaborates, from such a perspective (2001, 336): "Distinctions or concepts are system-internal constructions to which nothing in the world corresponds. It is not the nature of risk that dictates or corresponds to the use of the distinction between risk and certainty, but it is the use of the distinction between risk and certainty that determines the nature of risk. The nature of risk is determined by and changes with the nature of the distinction (risk/certainty or risk/danger) that is used to indicate the risk-side of the distinction."

9. Power's claim to investigate practices is somewhat compromised by near exclusive attention to systems of representation at the discursive level; he does not necessarily show *how* risk is produced by management systems, despite his emphasis on practice. I thank Martha Poon for passing along Power's book, from which I draw extensively. Her research (forthcoming) on the emergence of credit scores is a corrective to purely discursive analyses of the practice of risk.

10. Power's position is distinct from the influential work of Beck and Giddens, who both claim that risk defines the primary mode of contemporary sociopolitical organization, which is given the rather athletic title of "reflexive risk-modernity." They argue that "manufactured risk" and "reflexivity" are the de-

fining features of a new or "second" modernity, which, no longer defined by a reductionist belief in a linear and predictable future, entails an awareness of risk as a virtual contingency (cf. Giddens 1991; Beck 1992, 1999, 2008; Beck, Giddens, and Lash 1994). Power's account of the emergence of "rational designs for risk management" cannot be equated with these arguments for the increased "risk reflexivity" of individuals in a new "risk society." Not only does Power's rejection of the ontology of risk imply that one cannot easily claim that the world is objectively riddled by increased risk today, but his view is that Beck's idea of "risk society" appeals to contemporary anxieties. As he says (2007, 21), "Beck's ideas appeal in contexts where there is an increasing consciousness of self-produced risks and also doubts about the capacity of a flourishing risk regulation industry to cope with them." See also Smith and Tombs 2000; Arnoldi 2004 on Beck.

11. Faculties of universities will be familiar with these forms of self-challenging management practices, evidently put in place to encourage an ideal of self-overcoming. On risk as opportunity, see the references in Power 2007, especially O'Malley 2004. Cf. Millo and MacKenzie 2007 on financial risk management as a "boundary object," or a set of practices that serves communication and common operations between communities despite the lack of shared meaning between communities of practice. The authors argue that "as risk management became an integral part of common organizational market practices (e.g., margin calculation and intra-portfolio coordination), the actual content of the predictions that risk management systems produced became less relevant" (2). For an anthropological study of management systems, which generate practices that are translated into the terms of value, see Chong 2012.

12. Qualification should not be taken to signify "good" or "bad." The question is how something is qualified such that it can be classified, gradated, standardized, and hence quantified. The point that the coordinated assessment of qualities is necessary for calculation and exchange is made by scholars associated with the *"economie des conventions,"* or studies of multiple coexisting conventions of valuation: cf. Eymard-Duvernay 1989; Karpik 1989, 2007; Orléans 1994; Favereau, Biencourt, and Eymard-Duvernay 2002. For elaboration, and on the notion of markets as "calculative collective devices," see Callon 1998; Callon, Méadel, and Rabeharisoa 2002; Callon and Muniesa 2005; Muniesa 2007. Research on qualification as necessary to calculative agencies implies that algorithms and derivatives do not reduce life to mathematical operations, nor do they entail the mathematization of the life-world (cf. Lépinay 2011). More generally, cf. Bowker and Star 1999; Lampland and Star 2009.

13. This nutshell statement refers to performativity, as understood by Michel Callon, for whom financial devices are not used in contexts, but create contexts—the model and its context should be taken as an ontic state. The trans-

formation of context *for* the model is such that: "New adjustments are made; the formula is given a new twist (volatility skew) that translates into an alteration of the socio-technical *agencements* (dedicated professionals and observation tools are required to carry out the calculation of this parameter daily)" (Callon 2006, 15). For clarification of Callon's reference to performativity, cf. Callon 1998, 2010; and read MacKenzie 2003; MacKenzie, Muniesa, and Siu 2007. Some liberal economists put forth vague iterations of a similar point: Quantitative risk management systems tend "to signal increased risk just after a market crash rather than before it. The upshot of this process is that once an asset has already fallen sharply in price, the risk system will then adjust higher its estimate of the asset's likely range of returns, making the asset appear more risky after a sharp loss than before that loss" (Cooper 2008, 152). And cf. Soros (2009) on reflexivity in financial markets, or the idea that the processes of calculating risks and trading according to those calculations serves to transform the risks themselves.

14. Unfortunately, even most authors writing from the perspective of the social studies of finance are seduced by the race to explain the crisis and therefore sidestep the ways in which their own accountings of financial markets serve alternative, noncrisis social science narratives. But see Ortiz 2011, who notes that "an 'anthropology of the financial crisis' could not simply take the crisis for granted." Although he does not inquire into the term, Ortiz does raise questions about where and how one would define and locate financial crisis.

15. On this vision of economy, articulated by Gabriel Tarde, see Latour and Lépinay 2009.

16. The history of financial modeling is approached in terms of a concern for financial literacy by Mary Poovey and Kevin R. Brine in their forthcoming book.

17. I draw extensively from Martha Poon's remarkable research on financial innovation and commercial consumer credit. I am grateful to her for clarifying many points made herein.

18. This process cannot be reduced to a matter of mere technological diffusion because it entailed "continuous distribution, adaptation, discovery and innovation" (Poon 2009, 670).

19. "Within a proliferation of underwriting programs, algorithms, mortgage scores, ratings agencies, and lenders, for practical intents and purposes, in the mortgage industry, there are two independently functioning circuits of mortgage finance—the government sanctioned prime and the private label subprime. What divides them are information systems, their regard for risk, and product development; what unites them is a common reliance and baseline interpretation of FICO scores" (Poon 2009, 666). Because private-label subprime securities produced such great value, "the GSEs themselves were caught holding some $170 billion in private-label subprime securities, prod-

ucts which they never would have underwritten themselves. Like so many others, they had purchased these as investments because they were triple-A rated by the ratings agencies" (669).

20. Many look to nonregulated institutions and markets as sources of risk products. They point out, for instance, that the blue-chip corporation most famous for issuing these forms of insurance, AIG, was not subject to bank regulation and capital requirements, just as credit default swaps were not regulated as insurance. However, novel forms of arbitrage and wealth creation almost always emerge on the margins or outside the bounds of regulation and yet are dependent, in various ways, upon public or state infrastructures and initiatives (Roitman 2005; Palan 2006; Maurer 2008) or are novel techniques of self-regulation that are upheld by public law (Riles 2011)—all of which makes the public-private distinction irrelevant or heuristically unhelpful.

21. A general, methodological answer to this question is implicit in the particular, epistemological questions about "financial crisis" that I elaborate below. That general reply is best stated by Bruno Latour: "To convince the critically minded that constructivism means our only slow and progressive *access* to objectivity, morality, civil peace, and piety, and that, for this reason, all the subtle mediations of practice should be *protected* and cherished instead of being debunked and slowly destroyed would require such a deep alteration in our intellectual ecology that it is hard to see how it would come about" (2003, 42, emphasis in original).

22. Nouriel Roubini, "Ian Bremmer and Nouriel Roubini: Author One-to-One," *Editorial Reviews, Amazon.com Reviews* (August 9, 2010): accessed August 10, 2010, http://www.amazon.com/Crisis-Economics-Course-Future-Finance /dp/1594202508?tag=lipmon-20.

23. This causal argument runs throughout the examples set forth in the book; see, for example, Krippner 2011, 58–67 versus Riles 2011, who emphasizes the diffusion of a set of legal practices, which cannot be reduced to deregulation—to the contrary.

24. Cf. chapter 4, esp. p. 94, and chapter 6.

25. Annelise Riles (2011, 61) notes the problem of metaphor: "Contrary to industry executives' descriptions of the conditions that precipitated a need for government intervention as 'the perfect storm,' an 'act of god,' a 'tsunami,' and so on, such conditions are not at all unpredictable. As Katsunori Mikuniya, the commissioner of Japan's Financial Services Agency, wryly put it in a recent speech, 'While the current financial crisis has been described as a once-in-a-century credit tsunami, Tokyo, as a financial center, has experienced two tsunamis over the past decade.'"

26. While not an elaboration of that prospect, it is worth contemplating the fact that the Clinton administration commissioned a report, intended for inclusion in the "Economic Report of the President," entitled "Life after

Debt." Largely written in 2000 by the economist Jason Seligman, and never published, this "secret" report asks: "What would it look like to be in the United States without debt?" and "What would life look like in those United States?" These were not rhetorical questions. See the report by Planet Money (NPR blog), where the report can be accessed. http://www.npr.org /blogs/money/2011/10/21/141510617/what-if-we-paid-off-the-debt-the-secret -government-report, accessed October 20, 2010.

27. See Shank 2008 for commentary on Starn's writing on the epistemological status of the term "crisis" in historiography.

28. Starn refers to Thomas Kuhn, *The Structure of Scientific Revolutions* (1962) as an example of this use of crisis, which conveys processes of destruction and construction (anomaly and contingent) in the history of science.

29. To clarify, Munz argues, "in a properly intelligible narrative there is next to no contingency. This is not the same as saying that there is no contingency *res gestea*. It merely says that when we select particle events to join them with other particle events into a mininarrative, and so forth, we are always selecting in such a way as to extrude contingency. . . . The absence of contingency is not due to the presence of a development law anymore than it is due to the fact that there are no contingencies" (Munz 1977, 297). In what he sees as a companion piece to Hayden White's *Metahistory*, he nonetheless argues for a philosophy of history. Some might contend that Alain Badiou's notion of an event is distinct from that of Peter Munz's historiography or Hayden White's narratology, being extrinsic to ontology. However, if all events are ethical events, if one becomes a subject through the event, through the "truth procedures" of love, politics, art, science, or necessarily through "what makes the world a world *for us*, that is to say, a *meaningful* world" (Critchley 2001, 102), then this distinction deserves more thought.

30. The most recent flurry of social science writing on crisis—be that writing that assumes crisis as a condition or writing that investigates crisis as a condition—is surely also inspired by the translations and publications of Giorgio Agamben and the consequential fascination with Carl Schmitt. Most notably, various forms of incarceration—"the camp"—have been apprehended as instantiations of the sovereign's constitutive power to decide the exception. There is perhaps good reason for the appeal of Agamben and Schmitt for these interpretations: in the United States, the events of September 11, 2001, unleashed a great desire to examine and contest the consequences of a "state of emergency" and a "state of exception." The invocation of crisis served to legitimate the abridgment of constitutional rights and the institutionalization of extra-juridical executive powers. The notion of "the moment," however, has a long tradition of reflection in philosophy; see, for a short review in English, Friese 2001.

31. Vigh (2008) refers to Walter Benjamin's "state of emergency" in his defini-

tion of "crisis." See also Fassin and Pandolfi 2010. But see Collier and Lakoff (2008), who, in their work on the concepts and techniques that were elaborated in the theorization of "emergency situations" for United States civil defense programs in the 1950s, and the concomitant production of a consensus around the doctrine and ideal of the "national security state," note the inappropriate referencing of "states of exception" for situations that did not necessarily entail sovereign exception to extant legality. Alongside the passion for Schmidt and Agamben is the influence of Giddens and Beck, noted above.

32. Parrochia refers here to Durschmied 2000 on contingency.

33. It is worth comparing Giddens (1999) and Beck (1992) on risk society with regard to this point, and the rise of "mathematical ethics" as a form of judgment, without losing the point that Beck's apocalyptical vision is in direct confrontation with Parrochia's mathematical ethics.

34. Parrochia refers to Canguilhem's magnificent statement about the living being (*le vivant*) being in constant debate with its environment (*le milieu*), though he strangely ignores Canguilhem's contention (1966) that this debate is not a form of crisis; it is the ongoing production of new forms and states of normativity.

35. A crucial and opposing position is put forth by Elie Ayache in *The Blank Swan* (2010), his response to the overwhelmingly popular metaphor of the *Black Swan* (Taleb 2007). Interestingly, Ayache seeks to hold pricing, writing, and contingent claims on the same ontological level—to posit them as "events" outside of the realm of probability—outside of prediction. Here, he is in dialogue with Quentin Meillassoux (2008).

36. I thank Gil Anidjar for helping me to formulate the question in this way; for confirming that the recent work of Quentin Meillassoux (2008) is a crucial exploration of this very question, or the matter of positing a world absent of reason, from which we are exiled; and for suggesting that, in this sense, we are not exiled from history, but history is exile (see Raz-Krakotzkin 2007).

CONCLUSION: DREAMS

1. This describes the aims of narratives often described as "post-structuralist" or "postmodern," the expression "bearing witness to the differend" being that of Lyotard in *The Differend* (1988, xiii). The injunction to "witness" partakes of a Judeo-Christian genealogy that seeks to redeem what has been lost (or silenced, in Lyotard's language), though often according to an ethics of remembrance as opposed to emancipation. Furthermore, the notion that such accounts produce effects, such as the production of difference, while laudable (to my mind), is nonetheless a style of observation that is not particularly *post*modern. See Luhmann 2002, 189, and Rasch 2000, 84–123. Moreover, as Rabinow says (2008, 35), "But, as Weber hammered home a century ago,

to be conceptualized, tested and interpreted, things need to be identified as significant. And that nominalist task does not arise spontaneously from the things themselves. Or, as Geertz put it once, anthropologists study villages, good anthropologists study processes in villages. Choosing those processes is not mere witnessing but is itself an act of interpretation, or diagnosis." See also Rabinow 2003 on a nominalist sensibility.

2. A point made by scholars associated with constructivist theories, but see also Canguilhem 1988; Luhmann 1995, xli–xlii, and 115–66; Hacking 1999, 2004; Latour 1999b, 2003; Rabinow 2003; and Rabinow et al. 2008.

3. In related manner, Luhmann (1982, 119) argues that, because critique, as a "reflexive method for formulating values and norms" is fully institutionalized, terms such as "justice" and "truth" retain only symbolic functions. In that sense, the dichotomies that structure all social theory ensure the unity of allegedly rival approaches; transformation could only ensue by accounting for that unity.

4. For lack of space, I cannot multiply the examples, which would include the role of "crisis" in the elaboration of humanitarianism and its associated ethic of witnessing (cf. Redfield 2005, 2006 and Roitman forthcoming). For a critique of Habermas's distinction between system and life-world, which leads to a similar narration in terms of failure, cf. Knodt 1994, 2010.

5. It would be worth considering the narrative forms that crisis enables, as suggested with humor though not entirely pursued with force by Joshua Clover (2011): "In the early days of the crisis everything was written on the waters, shifting moment to moment. Most eloquent was the mercurial renaming of 2008's investor panic. Toward what did we flee? The word 'safety' was swiftly deemed too suggestive of danger; the subsequent 'liquidity' sounded a bit technical; by general agreement, we settled on the lullaby of 'quality.' *Flight to safety, flight to liquidity, flight to quality*: If you spot in this something of the epic, you are not mistaken. Indeed, this sequence is a fine thumbnail of *The Aeneid*, as our hero flees the burning city of Troy, scuds across the seas, and eventually arrives at Rome. Option-ARMS and the man I sing." Clover concludes:

> Flight to safety, flight to liquidity, flight to quality. The flight has begun; this much is true. But we are not adrift on the tides of investor risk preferences; we are on the seas of history, between the great swells of empire. This has always been the true significance of the epic. It tells the story of transformation between capitals; the gods play the part of destiny, the unseen inner logic of the world-system, into which the hero is tossed in need of a home. However, this takes on a different substance in an epoch when we have reached the limits of the globe, when there is no unfound Rome on which to found a new empire, and the familiar dynamic has run its course. We fancy ourselves done with the gods; are we equally as free

from the thrall of destiny, from a systemic dynamic that remains alien to us? And is this not what we should be debating, rather than the merits of management styles for the old capital?

He thus raises the question of the significance of the epic form of narration and the thrall of the concept of destiny, which serves a philosophy of history, but he then reinscribes this form and that philosophy in the problem of humanity's alienation from history precisely because of his own accession to crisis.

6. "If a knowing system has no entry to its external world it can be denied that such an external world exists. But we can just as well—and more believably—claim that the external world is as it is. Neither claim can be proved; there is no way of deciding between them" (Luhmann 1990a, 67). Again, my intention is not to designate "crisis" as either "real" or "error" since, following Luhmann: "the predicate 'real' can no longer simply be attributed, or (in the case of error) denied, to what is designated. The value of reality shifts from the designation (reference) to the distinction that is co-actualized in every designation. Real is what is practiced as a distinction, what is taken apart by it, what is made visible and invisible by it: the world." One can only be struck by the recursivity of this statement when taken in consideration of the term "crisis." Because "knowing" is necessarily a self-referential process, my work on "crisis" can be qualified as redistributive: there are no exempt positions in a system of recursive observations (see Knodt 1994, 92, quoting Luhmann). If competing descriptions of the world are incommensurate or, better, equally valid, the problem is not necessarily to accept one over the other but rather to accept the very necessity of competing contingency, which is then not a "crisis," as Megill (1985, 2007), for instance, claims. Cf. Christis (2001) on Luhmann and skepticism or nihilism. More generally, among many others, see Bernstein 1983, 2010; Putnam 1995, 2002; Hacking 1999, 2004; Latour 2003.

7. A dilemma that is referred to throughout this book, though will not be rehearsed here. See, among the countless publications, the writings of Benjamin, Gadamer, Ricoeur, and Derrida; and refer to White 1973, 1978; and Clifford and Marcus 1986.

8. Apart from the work of Deleuze, Derrida, and Bergson, a few examples of these attempts include Haraway 1991; Taussig 1993; Massumi 2002; Bowker 2005; and Thrift 2008. Examples from media studies and creative practice or visualization in design studies are not known to me; but see Wark 2006 [2007] and Halpern forthcoming. It is claimed that nonrepresentational theory, "does not refuse representation per se, only representation as the repetition of the same or representation as mediation" (Anderson and Harrison 2010), which leaves untouched the question of linear narration typical to the essay or the book.

9. I do not have pretense to consider myself among the philosophically oriented anthropologists, but I do share Rabinow's goal of our labor as anthropologists.

10. For Rabinow, this inquiry entails an anthropology of the contemporary, distinct from a history of the present. See Rabinow 2003, 2008.

11. One possible form of inquiry that proceeds from these questions is expressed in Meillassoux 2008, though his work is not anthropological in the sense intended by Rabinow.

12. I repeat James Dodd's question regarding Husserl's work on crisis. As an aside, and without being "for" gas emissions or holes in the ozone, one could put this question to propositions regarding environmental crisis. For indications as to what such a project might look like, cf. Garrison 1981, 135–43; O'Connor 1988; Davis 1999.

13. This question echoes those posed by Mahatma Gandhi regarding his "politics of accord" (cf. Gandhi 2011).

14. Or crisis signifies a veritable aporia: an impasse in speaking, writing, narration, and the *inability* to bear witness. See LaCapra 2004, 144–94. We could not narrate it.

15. See the DC comics edited edition of the classic 1985 *Crisis on Infinite Earths* (Wolfman and Perez 2001). It would be worth linking this point about narrative paradox in Superman to Hayden White's writing on the ironic apprehension of the relativism of knowledge (1973, 1978). And many will see resonances with Walter Benjamin's messianic time.

16. Blumenberg's reference is Voltaire's *Micromégas* (1752).

REFERENCES

Acharya, V. V., M. Richardson, S. van Nieuwerburgh, and L. J. White. 2011. *Guaranteed to Fail: Fannie Mae, Freddie Mac and the Debacle of Mortgage Finance.* Princeton, NJ: Princeton University Press.

Acton, H. B. 1975. Introduction to Hegel's *Natural Law*. Philadelphia: University of Pennsylvania Press.

Adam, B. 1995. *Timewatch: The Social Analysis of Time.* Cambridge: Polity Press.

——. 2004. *Time.* Cambridge: Polity Press.

Adam, B., and C. Groves. 2007. *Future Matters: Action, Knowledge, Ethics.* Boston: Brill.

Adorno, T. 1973. *Negative Dialectics.* London: Routledge.

Akerlof, G., and R. Shiller. 2009. *Animal Spirits: How Human Psychology Drives the Economy, and Why It Matters for Global Capitalism.* Princeton, NJ: Princeton University Press.

Anderson, B., and P. Harrison, eds. 2010. *Taking-Place: Non-Representational Theories and Geography.* London: Ashgate.

Anidjar, G. 2006. "Secularism." *Critical Inquiry* 33 (1): 52–77.

Appadurai, A. 1986. *The Social Life of Things: Commodities in Cultural Perspective.* Cambridge: Cambridge University Press.

Arnoldi, J., ed. 2001. Special issue on N. Luhmann. *Theory, Culture and Society* 18 (1).

——. 2004. "Derivatives: Virtual Values and Real Risks." *Theory, Culture and Society* 21 (6): 23–42.

Arrighi, G. 1994. *The Long Twentieth Century: Money Power, and the Origins of Our Times.* New York: Verso.

Arrighi, G., and B. Silver. 1999. *Chaos and Governance in the Modern World System.* Minneapolis: University of Minnesota Press.

Asad, T. 1993. *Genealogies of Religion: Discipline and Reasons of Power in Christianity and Islam.* Baltimore: Johns Hopkins University Press.

———. 1998. *Anthropology and the Colonial Encounter.* Amherst, NY: Humanity Books.

———. 2003. *Formations of the Secular: Christianity, Islam, Modernity.* Stanford, CA: Stanford University Press.

———. 2008. "Is Critique Secular? Historical Notes on the Idea of Secular Criticism." *The Immanent Frame* (SSRC blog), January 25. Accessed November 17, 2008. http://www.ssrc.org./blogs/immanent_frame/2008/01/25/historical-notes-on-the-idea.

Ayache, E. 2010. *The Blank Swan: The End of Probability.* Chichester, West Sussex, UK: John Wiley and Sons.

Baker, T., and J. Simon, eds. 2002. *Embracing Risk: The Changing Culture of Insurance and Responsibility.* Chicago: University of Chicago Press.

Balibar, E. 2012. *Europe: Crise et fin?* Paris: Broché.

Barry, A., T. Osborne, and N. Rose, eds. 1996. *Foucault and Political Reason: Liberalism, Neo-Liberalism, and Rationalities of Government.* Chicago: University of Chicago Press.

Beck, U. 1992. *Risk Society: Towards a New Modernity.* London: Sage.

———. 1999. *World Risk Society.* Malden, MA: Polity Press.

———. 2008. *World at Risk.* Cambridge: Polity Press.

Beck, U., A. Giddens, and S. Lash. 1994. *Reflexive Modernization: Politics, Tradition and Aesthetics in the Modern Social Order.* Cambridge: Polity Press.

Beckert, J., and P. Aspers. 2011. *The Worth of Goods: Valuation and Pricing in the Economy.* Oxford: Oxford University Press.

Beckett, G. 2008. "The End of Haiti: History under Conditions of Impossibility." PhD diss., Department of Anthropology, University of Chicago.

Béjin, A., and E. Morin, eds. 1976. "La notion de crise." Centre d'études transdisciplinaires, *Communication* 25.

Bender, J., and D. Wellbery, eds. 1991. *Chronotypes: The Construction of Time.* Stanford, CA: Stanford University Press.

Benhabib, S. 1986. *Critique, Norm, and Utopia.* New York: Columbia University Press.

Benjamin, W. 1968. *Illuminations.* New York: Schocken Books.

Bernstein, P. 1996a. *Against the Gods: The Remarkable Story of Risk.* New York: John Wiley and Sons.

———. 1996b. "The New Religion of Risk Management." *Harvard Business Review* 74 (2): 47–51.

Bernstein, R. 1983. *Beyond Objectivism and Relativism: Science, Hermeneutics, and Praxis.* Philadelphia: University of Pennsylvania Press.

————. 2010. *The Pragmatic Turn*. Cambridge: Polity Press.

Beunza, D., I. Hardie, and D. MacKenzie. 2006. "A Price Is a Social Thing: Towards a Material Sociology of Arbitrage." *Organization Studies* 27: 721–45.

Bhargava, R. 1998. *Secularism and Its Critics*. New York: Oxford University Press.

Biddick, K. 2003. *The Typological Imaginary*. Philadelphia: University of Pennsylvania Press.

Bilgrami, A. 2006. *Self-Knowledge and Resentment*. Cambridge, MA: Harvard University Press.

Bloor, D. 1991. *Knowledge and Social Imaginary*. Chicago: University of Chicago Press.

————. 1999a. "Anti-Latour." *Studies in History and Philosophy of Science* 30 (1): 81–112.

————. 1999b. "Reply to Bruno Latour." *Studies in History and Philosophy of Science* 30 (1): 131–36.

————. 2001. "Wittgenstein and the Priority of Practice." In *The Practice Turn in Contemporary Theory*, edited by K. Knorr-Cetina, T. R. Schatzki, and E. von Savigny, 95–106. London: Routledge.

Blumenberg, H. [1966] 1983. *The Legitimacy of the Modern Age*. Cambridge: MIT Press.

————. [1979] 1997. *Shipwreck with Spectator*. Cambridge: MIT Press.

————. 2010. *Care Crosses the River*. Stanford, CA: Stanford University Press.

Boas, F. 1966. *Race, Language, and Culture*. New York: Free Press.

Boland, T. 2007. "Critique as a Technique of Self: A Butlerian Analysis of Judith Butler's Prefaces." *History of the Human Sciences* 20 (3): 105–22.

Boltanski, L., and L. Thévenot. 1991. *De la justification*. Paris: Gallimard.

Bookstaber, R. 2007. *A Demon of Our Own Design: Markets, Hedge Funds, and the Perils of Financial Innovation*. Hoboken, NJ: John Wiley and Sons.

Bowker, G. 2005. *Memory Practices in the Sciences*. Cambridge: MIT Press.

Bowker, G., and S. L. Star. 1999. *Sorting Things Out: Classification and Its Consequences*. Cambridge: MIT Press.

Braithwaite, T. 2011. "US Panel's Report Reflects Partisan Rift." *Financial Times*, posted online January 30, 2011. http://www.ft.com.

Brenner, N., and N. Theodore, eds. 2002. *Spaces of Neoliberalism: Urban Restructuring in North America and Western Europe*. Malden, MA: Blackwell.

Brenner, R. 2002. *The Boom and the Bubble*. London: Verso.

————. 2006. *The Economics of Global Turbulence*. London: Verso.

Browne, C. 2008. "The End of Immanent Critique?" *European Journal of Social Theory* 11: 5–24.

Brunner, O., W. Conze, and R. Koselleck, eds. 1972–97. *Geschichtliche Grundbegriffe. Historisches Lexikon zur politisch-sozialen in Deutschland*. Stuttgart, Germany: Klett.

Bryan, D., and M. Rafferty. 2006. *Capitalism with Derivatives: A Political Economy of Financial Derivatives, Capital and Class.* Basingstoke, UK: Palgrave Macmillan.

———. 2007. "Financial Derivatives and the Theory of Money." *Economy and Society* 36 (1): 134–58.

Burke, K. 1969. *A Grammar of Motives.* Berkeley: University of California Press.

Butler, J. 1993. *Bodies That Matter: On the Discursive Limits of "Sex."* New York: Routledge.

———. 1999. *Subjects of Desire: Hegelian Reflections in Twentieth-Century France.* New York: Columbia University Press.

———. 2002. "What Is Critique? An Essay on Foucault's Virtue." In *The Political: Readings in Continental Philosophy*, edited by D. Ingram, 212–28. London: Basil Blackwell.

———. 2004. *The Judith Butler Reader.* Malden, MA: Blackwell.

Butterfield, J., ed. 1999. *The Arguments of Time.* New York: Oxford University Press.

Calhoun, C. 2011. "From the Current Crisis to Possible Futures." In *Business as Usual: The Roots of the Global Financial Meltdown*, edited by C. Calhoun and G. Derluguian, 9–42. New York: New York University Press.

Calhoun, C., and G. Derluguian, eds. 2011. *Business as Usual: The Roots of the Global Financial Meltdown.* New York: New York University Press.

Çalışkan, K. 2010. *Market Threads: How Farmers and Traders Create a Global Economy.* Princeton, NJ: Princeton University Press.

Çalışkan, K., and M. Callon. 2009. "Economization, Part 1: Shifting Attention from the Economy towards Processes of Economization." *Economy and Society* 38 (3): 369–98.

———. 2010. "Economization, Part 2: A Research Programme for the Study of Markets." *Economy and Society* 39 (1): 1–32.

Callon, M. 1998. *The Laws of the Markets.* London: Blackwell.

———. 2006. "What Does It Mean to Say That Economics Is Performative?" CSI Working Papers Series, Number 005. Paris: Centre de Sociologie de l'Innovation.

———. 2010. "Performativity, Misfires and Politics." *Journal of Cultural Economy* 3 (2): 163–69.

Callon, M., and B. Latour. 1981. "Unscrewing the Big Leviathans: How Do Actors Macrostructure Reality?" In *Advances in Social Theory and Methodology: Toward an Integration of Micro and Macro Sociologies*, edited by K. Knorr and A. Cicourel. London: Routledge.

Callon, M., C. Méadel, and V. Rabeharisoa. 2002. "The Economy of Qualities." *Economy and Society* 31 (2): 194–217.

Callon, M., Y. Millo, and F. Muniesa, eds. 2007. *Market Devices.* Oxford: Blackwell Publishing.

Callon, M., and F. Muniesa. 2005. "Economic Markets as Calculative and Calculated Collective Devices." *Organizational Studies* 26 (8): 1229–50.

Canguilhem, G. 1966. *Le normal et le pathologique*. Paris: Presses Universitaires
de France.

———. 1988. *Ideology and Rationality in the History of the Life Sciences*. Cambridge: MIT Press.

Carr, D. 1987. Book Review: Koselleck, *Futures Past*. *History and Theory* 26 (2):
197–204.

———. 1999. *The Paradox of Subjectivity: The Self in the Transcendental Tradition*.
New York: Oxford University Press.

Carruthers, G., and A. Stinchcombe. 1999. "The Social Structure of Liquidity:
Flexibility in Markets and States." *Theory and Society* 28 (3): 353–82.

Chakrabarty, D. 2000. *Provincializing Europe: Postcolonial Thought and Historical
Difference*. Princeton, NJ: Princeton University Press.

Chong, K. 2012. *The Work of Financialisation: An Ethnography of a Global Management Consultancy in Post-Mao China*. Unpublished doctoral dissertation. Department of Anthropology, London School of Economics.

Chorev, N. 2010. "On the Origins of Neoliberalism: Political Shifts and Analytical Challenges." In *Handbook of Politics: State and Society in Global Perspective*,
edited by K. Leicht and C. Jenkins, part 1: 127–44. New York: Springer.

Christis, J. 2001. "Luhmann's Theory of Knowledge: Beyond Realism and Constructivism?" *Soziale Systeme* 7, Heft 2: 328–49.

Clarke, J. 2010. "After Neo-Liberalism? Markets, States and the Reinvention of
Public Welfare." *Cultural Studies* 24 (3): 375–94.

Clarke, N. 2009. "In What Sense 'Space of Neoliberalism'? The New Localism,
The New Politics of Scale, and Town Twinning." *Political Geography* 28 (8):
496–507.

Clifford, J., and G. Marcus, eds. 1986. *Writing Culture*. Berkeley: University of
California Press.

Clover, J. 2011. "Autumn of the Empire." *Los Angeles Review of Books* (online
edition), July 18. http://lareviewofbooks.org/post/7756129051/autumn-of
-the-empire.

Cohan, W. 2009. *House of Cards: A Tale of Hubris and Wretched Excess on Wall
Street*. New York: Doubleday.

Cohn, J. [1896] 1994. *Histoire de l'infini*. Paris: Les Editions du Cerf.

Collier, S. 2011. *Post-Soviet Social: Neoliberalism, Social Modernity, Biopolitics*.
Princeton, NJ: Princeton University Press.

Collier, S., and A. Lakoff. 2008. "Distributed Preparedness: The Spatial Logic of
Domestic Security in the United States." *Environment and Planning D: Society
and Space* 26 (1): 7–28.

Cooper, G. 2008. *The Origin of Financial Crises: Central Banks, Credit Bubbles and
the Efficient Market Fallacy*. New York: Vintage Books.

Critchley, S. 1999. "Introduction: What Is Continental Philosophy?" In *A Companion to Continental Philosophy*, edited by S. Critchley and W. R. Schroeder, 1–17. Malden, MA: Wiley-Blackwell.

———. 2001. "On Alain Badiou." In *The Moment. Time and Rupture in Modern Thought*, edited by H. Friese, 91–111. Liverpool, UK: Liverpool University Press.

———. 2007. *Infinitely Demanding*. New York: Verso.

Daston, L. 1988. *Classical Probability in the Enlightenment*. Princeton, NJ: Princeton University Press.

Davis, K. 2008. *Periodization and Sovereignty: How Ideas of Feudalism and Secularization Govern the Politics of Time*. Philadelphia: University of Pennsylvania Press.

Davis, M. 1999. *Ecology of Fear. Los Angeles and the Imagination of Disaster*. New York: Vintage Books.

Deleuze, G. 1994. *Difference and Repetition*. New York: Columbia University Press.

Deleuze, G., and F. Guattari. 1996. *What Is Philosophy?* New York: Columbia University Press.

de Vries, H., and L. Sullivan. 2006. *Political Theologies: Public Religions in a Post Secular World*. New York: Fordham University Press.

Doane, M. 2002. *The Emergence of Cinematic Time*. Cambridge, MA: Harvard University Press.

Dodd, J. 2004. *Crisis and Reflection: An Essay on Husserl's Crisis of the European Sciences*. Dordrecht, the Netherlands: Kluwer Academic Publishers.

Duménil, G., and D. Lévy. 2011. *The Crisis of Neoliberalism*. Cambridge, MA: Harvard University Press.

Durschmied, E. 2000. *La logique du grain de sable, quand la chance ou l'incompétence ont changé le cours de l'histoire*. Paris: J.-C. Lattès/Trinacra.

Eco, U. 1984. "The Myth of Superman." In *The Role of the Reader*, 107–24. Bloomington: Indiana University Press.

Edwards, J. 2006. "*Critique and Crisis* Today: Koselleck, Enlightenment and the Concept of Politics." *Contemporary Political Theory* 5: 428–46.

Elyachar, J. 2005. *Markets of Dispossession: NGOs, Economic Development, and the State*. Durham, NC: Duke University Press.

———. 2012. "Before (and After) Neoliberalism: Tacit Knowledge, Secrets of the Trade, and the Public Sector in Egypt." *Cultural Anthropology* 27 (1): 76–96.

Ermarth, E. 1992. *Sequel to History: Postmodernism and the Crisis of Representational Time*. Princeton, NJ: Princeton University Press.

Eymard-Duvernay, F. 1989. "Conventions de qualité et formes de coordination." *Revue économique* 40 (2): 329–59.

Fabian, J. 1983. *Time and the Other: How Anthropology Makes Its Objects*. New York: Columbia University Press.

Fassin, D., and M. Pandolfi, eds. 2010. *Contemporary States of Emergency: The Politics of Military and Humanitarian Interventions*. Brooklyn, NY: Zone Books.

Favereau, O., O. Biencourt, and F. Eymard-Duvernay. 2002. "Where Do Markets Come From? From (Quality) Conventions!" In *Conventions and Structures in Economic Organizations: Markets, Networks and Hierarchies*, edited by O. Favereau and E. Lazega, 213–48. Cheltenham, UK: Edward Elgar Publishing.

Fligstein, N. 2005. "The End of (Shareholder Value) Ideology?" In *Political Power and Social Theory*, vol. 17, edited by D. Davis, 223–28. Bingley, UK: Emerald.

Foster, J., and F. Magdoff. 2009. *The Great Financial Crisis: Causes and Consequences*. New York: Monthly Review Press.

Foucault, M. 1970. *The Order of Things: An Archaeology of the Human Sciences*. New York: Pantheon Books.

———. 1972. *The Archeology of Knowledge and the Discourse on Language*. New York: Pantheon Books.

———. 1973. *The Order of Things. An Archaeology of the Human Sciences*. New York: Vintage Books.

———. 1980. *Power/Knowledge: Selected Interviews and Other Writings 1972–1977*. Edited by C. Gorden. New York: Pantheon.

———. 1985. *The Use of Pleasure: History of Sexuality*. Vol. 2. New York: Vintage Press.

———. 1997a. "What Is Critique?" In *The Politics of Truth*, edited by S. Lotringer and L. Hochroth, 41–82. New York: Semiotext(e).

———. 1997b. "What Is Enlightenment?" In *Ethics, Subjectivity and Truth. Essential Works of Foucault 1954–1984*, edited by P. Rabinow, 1: 303–19. New York: New Press.

Fox, J. 2009. *The Myth of the Rational Market: A History of Risk, Reward, and Delusion on Wall Street*. New York: HarperCollins.

Franklin, J. ed. 1998. *The Politics of Risk Society*. Malden, MA: Polity Press.

Friese, H. 2001. *The Moment: Time and Rupture in Modern Thought*. Liverpool, UK: Liverpool University Press.

Fuchs, S. 1996. "The New Wars of Truth: Conflicts over Science Studies as Differentiated Modes of Observation." *Social Science Information* 35 (2): 307–26.

Furet, F. 1978. *Penser la Révolution française*. Paris: Gallimard.

———. 1981. *Interpreting the French Revolution*. Cambridge: Cambridge University Press.

Gandhi, L. 2011. "The Pauper's Give: Postcolonial Theory and the New Democratic Dispensation." *Public Culture* 23 (1): 27–38.

Garland, D. 2003. "The Rise of Risk." In *Risk and Morality*, edited by R. Ericson and A. Doyle, 48–86. Toronto: University of Toronto Press.

Garrison, C. 1981. "The Energy Crisis: A Process of Social Definition." *Qualitative Sociology* 4 (4): 312–23.

Giddens, A. 1991. *Modernity and Self-Identity*. Stanford, CA: Stanford University Press.

———. 1999. "Risk and Responsibility." *Modern Law Review* 62 (January): 1–10.

———. 2003. *Runaway World: How Globalization Is Reshaping Our Lives*. London: Routledge.

Gorton, G. 2010. *Slapped by the Invisible Hand: The Panic of 2007*. New York: Oxford University Press.

Gourevitch, V. 1998. Preface to R. Koselleck, *Critique and Crisis: Enlightenment and the Pathogenesis of Modern Society*. Cambridge, MA: Berg Publishers.

Greenhouse, C., E. Mertz, and K. Warren. eds. 2002. *Ethnography in Unstable Places: Everyday Lives in Contexts of Dramatic Political Change*. Durham, NC: Duke University Press.

Greenspan, A. 2007. *The Age of Turbulence: Adventures in a New World*. New York: Penguin.

———. 2010. *The Crisis*. Brookings Papers on Economic Activity (Spring): 201–61. http://www.brookings.edu/~/media/Files/Programs/ES/BPEA/2010_spring_bpea_papers/spring2010_greenspan.pdf.

Grim, P. 1991. *The Incomplete Universe: Totality, Knowledge, and Truth*. Cambridge: MIT Press.

Grossberg, L. 2007. "Rereading the Past from the Future." *International Journal of Cultural Studies* 10 (1): 125–33.

———. 2010. "Modernity and Commensuration." *Cultural Studies* 24 (3): 295–332.

Grosz, E., ed. 1999. *Becomings: Explorations in Time, Memory, and Futures*. Ithaca, NY: Cornell University Press.

Gudeman, S. 2001. *The Anthropology of Economy: Community, Market, and Culture*. Malden, MA: Blackwell.

Guyer, J. 1995. *Money Matters: Instability, Values, and Social Payments in the Modern History of West Africa*. Portsmouth, NH: Heinemann.

———. 2004. *Marginal Gains: Monetary Transactions in Atlantic Africa*. Chicago: University of Chicago Press.

Habermas, J. 1975. *Legitimation Crisis*. New York: Beacon Press.

———. 1982. "A Reply to My Critics." In *Habermas: Critical Debates*, edited by J. B. Thompson and D. Held, 219–83. London: Macmillan.

———. 1984–87. *The Theory of Communicative Action*. 2 volumes. Boston: Beacon Press.

———. 1987. *The Philosophical Discourse of Modernity*. Cambridge: MIT Press.

Hacking, I. 1975. *The Emergence of Probability: A Philosophical Study of Early Ideas about Probability, Induction and Statistical Inference*. Cambridge: Cambridge University Press.

———. 1990. *The Taming of Chance*. Cambridge: Cambridge University Press.

———. 1999. *The Social Construction of What?* Cambridge, MA: Harvard University Press.

———. 2003. "Risk and Dirt." In *Risk and Morality*, edited by R. Ericson and A. Doyle, 22–47. Toronto: University of Toronto Press.

———. 2004. *Historical Ontology*. Cambridge, MA: Harvard University Press.

Halpern, O. Forthcoming. *Beautiful Data: A History of Vision and Reason since 1945*. Durham, NC: Duke University Press.

Hansen, D. 2005. *The Dream: Martin Luther King, Jr., and the Speech That Inspired a Nation*. New York: HarperCollins.

Haraway, D. 1991. *Simians, Cyborgs and Women: The Reinvention of Nature*. London: Free Association Books.

Hardt, M., and A. Negri. 2000. *Empire*. Cambridge, MA: Harvard University Press.

———. 2009. *Commonwealth*. Cambridge, MA: Belknap Press of Harvard University Press.

Hart, K. 1986. "Heads or Tails? Two Sides of the Coin." *Man* 21 (4): 637–56.

———. 2000. *The Memory Bank: Money in an Unequal World*. Cheshire, UK: Texere.

Hartman, Y. 2005. "In Bed with the Enemy: Some Ideas on the Connections between Neoliberalism and the Welfare State." *Current Sociology* 53 (January): 57–73.

Harvey, D. 2003. *The New Imperialism*. New York: Oxford University Press.

———. 2005. *A Brief History of Neoliberalism*. New York: Oxford University Press.

———. 2010. *The Enigma of Capital: And the Crises of Capitalism*. New York: Oxford University Press.

———. 2011. "The Enigma of Capital and the Crisis This Time." In *Business as Usual: The Roots of the Global Financial Meltdown*, edited by C. Calhoun and G. Derluguian, 89–112. New York: NYU Press.

Hay, J. 2010. "Too Good to Fail: Managing Financial Crisis through the Moral Economy of Reality TV." *Journal of Communication Inquiry* 34 (4): 382–402.

Hayden, C. 2003. *When Nature Goes Public: The Making and Unmaking of Bioprospecting in Mexico*. Princeton, NJ: Princeton University Press.

Hayward, M. 2010. "The Economic Crisis and After: Recovery, Reconstruction and Cultural Studies." *Cultural Studies* 24 (3): 283–94.

Hobbes, T. [1651] 1994. *Leviathan*. Indianapolis: Hackett Publishing.

Hoffman, S., and A. Oliver-Smith, eds. 2002. *Catastrophe and Culture: The Anthropology of Disaster*. Santa Fe, NM: School of American Research Press.

Hoffmeyer, J. 1994. *The Advent of Freedom*. Cranbury, NJ: Associated University Press.

Hopwood, A. G., and P. Miller, eds. 1994. *Accounting as Social and Institutional Practice*. Cambridge: Cambridge University Press.

Horkheimer, M. 1974. *Eclipse of Reason*. New York: Continuum.

Hoy, D. 2009. *The Time of Our Lives: A Critical History of Temporality*. Cambridge: MIT Press.

Husserl, E. [1954] 1970. *The Crisis of European Sciences and Transcendental Phenomenology*, translated by D. Carr. Evanston, IL: Northwestern University Press.

Jacobs, R. 1996. "Producing the News, Producing the Crisis: Narrativity, Television and News Work." *Media, Culture, and Society* 18: 373–97.

Jameson, F. 2002. *A Singular Modernity: Essay on the Ontology of the Present*. New York: Verso.

Jasanoff, S. 1994. *Learning from Disaster: Risk Management after Bhopal*. Philadelphia: University of Pennsylvania Press.

Jessop, B. 2000. "The Crisis of the National Spatio-Temporal Fix and the Tendential Ecological Dominance of Globalizing Capitalism." *International Journal of Urban and Regional Research* 24 (2): 323–60.

———. 2002. *The Future of the Capitalist State*. Cambridge: Cambridge University Press.

Johnson, S., and J. Kwak. 2010. *Bankers: The Wall Street Takeover and the Next Financial Meltdown*. New York: Pantheon Books.

Karpik, L. 1989. "L'économie de la qualité." *Revue Française de la Sociologie* 30: 187–210.

———. 2007. *L'Économie des singularités*. Paris: Broché.

Keane, W. 2001. "Money Is No Object: Materiality, Desire and Modernity in an Indonesian Society." In *The Empire of Things: Regimes of Values and Material Cultures*, edited by F. Myers, 65–90. Oxford: School of American Research Press.

Khan, N., ed. 2009. *Beyond Crisis: Re-evaluating Pakistan*. London: Routledge.

Knights, D., and T. Vurdubakis. 1993. "Calculations of Risk: Towards an Understanding of Insurance as a Moral and Political Technology." *Accounting, Organisations and Society* 19 (7–8): 729–64.

Knodt, E. 1994. "Toward a Non-Foundationalist Epistemology: The Habermas Luhmann Controversy Revisited." *New German Critique* 61: 77–100.

Koselleck, R. [1959] 1988. *Critique and Crisis: Enlightenment and the Pathogenesis of Modern Society*. Cambridge, MA: Berg Publishers.

———. 2002. *The Practices of Conceptual History: Timing History, Spacing Concepts*. Stanford, CA: Stanford University Press.

———. [1979] 2004. *Futures Past: On the Semantics of Historical Time*. New York: Columbia University Press.

———. [1972–97] 2006. "Crisis." *Journal of the History of Ideas* 67 (2): 357–400.

Koyre, A. 1957. *From the Closed World to the Infinite Universe*. Baltimore, MD: Johns Hopkins University Press.

Krippner, G. 2011. *Capitalizing on Crisis: The Political Origins of the Rise of Finance*. Cambridge, MA: Harvard University Press.

Krugman, P. 2007. "Innovating Our Way to Financial Crisis." *New York Times*, December 3. Accessed December 3, 2007. http://www.nytimes.com.

———. 2009. *The Return of Depression Economics and the Crisis of 2008*. New York: W. W. Norton.

Kuhn, T. 1962. *The Structure of Scientific Revolutions*. Chicago: University of Chicago Press.

LaCapra, D. 2004. *History in Transit*. Ithaca, NY: Cornell University Press.

Lampland, M., and S. L. Star. 2009. *Standards and Their Stories: How Quantifying, Classifying, and Formalizing Practices Shape Everyday Life*. Ithaca, NY: Cornell University Press.

Langley, P. 2008. "Sub-prime Mortgage Lending: A Cultural Economy." *Economy and Society* 37 (4): 469–94.

Latour, B. 1993. *We Have Never Been Modern*. Cambridge, MA: Harvard University Press.

———. 1996. *Aramis or the Love of Technology*. Cambridge, MA: Harvard University Press.

———. 1999a. "For David Bloor . . . and Beyond: A Reply to David Bloor's 'Anti Latour.'" *Studies in History and Philosophy of Science* 30 (1): 113–29.

———. 1999b. *Pandora's Hope*. Cambridge, MA: Harvard University Press.

———. 2003. "The Promises of Constructivism." In *Chasing Technoscience*, edited by D. Ihde and E. Selinger, 27–46. Bloomington: Indiana University Press.

———. 2004. "Why Has Critique Run Out of Steam? From Matters of Fact to Matters of Concern." *Critical Inquiry* 30 (winter): 225–48.

———. 2005. *Reassembling the Social: An Introduction to Actor-Network Theory*. New York: Oxford University Press.

Latour, B., and V. Lépinay. 2009. *The Science of Passionate Interests: An Introduction to Gabriel Tarde's Economic Anthropology*. Chicago: Prickly Paradigm Press.

La Volpa, A. 1992. "Conceiving a Public: Ideas and Society in Eighteenth-Century Europe." *Journal of Modern History* 64 (1): 79–116.

Lépinay, V. 2011. *Codes of Finance: Engineering Derivatives in a Global Bank*. Princeton, NJ: Princeton University Press.

Le Poidevin, R. 2003. *Travels in Four Dimensions. The Enigmas of Space and Time*. Oxford: Oxford University Press.

———. 2007. *The Images of Time: An Essay on Temporal Representation*. Oxford: Oxford University Press.

Lewis, M. 2010. *The Big Short: Inside the Doomsday Machine*. New York: W. W. Norton.

Lilla, M. 2007. *The Stillborn God: Religion, Politics and the Modern West*. New York: Alfred Knopf.

LiPuma, E., and B. Lee. 2004. *Financial Derivatives and the Globalization of Risk.* Durham, NC: Duke University Press.

Lo, A. 2012. "Reading about the Financial Crisis: A Twenty-One-Book Review." *Journal of Economic Literature* 50 (1): 151–78.

Loewenstein, B. 1976. "Book Review: Koselleck, *Kritik und Krise.*" *Journal of Modern History* 48 (1): 122–24.

Lomnitz, C. 2003. "Times of Crisis: Historicity, Sacrifice, and the Spectacle of Debacle in Mexico City." *Public Culture* 15 (1): 127–47.

Lordon, F. 2009. *La Crise de Trop: Reconstruction d'un monde failli.* Paris: Fayard.

Lovejoy, A. [1936] 1976. *The Great Chain of Being.* Cambridge, MA: Harvard University Press.

Löwith, K. 1949. *Meaning in History: The Theological Implications of the Philosophy of History.* Chicago: University of Chicago Press.

Luhmann, N. 1982. *The Differentiation of Society.* New York: Columbia University Press.

———. 1990a. "The Cognitive Program of Constructivism and a Reality That Remains Unknown." In *Self-organization: Portrait of a Scientific Revolution,* edited by W. Krohn, 64–85. Dordrecht, the Netherlands: Kluwer.

———. 1990b. *Essays on Self-Reference.* New York: Columbia University Press.

———. 1993. *Risk: A Sociological Theory.* New Brunswick, NJ: Transaction Publishers.

———. [1984] 1995. *Social Systems.* Stanford, CA: Stanford University Press.

———. [1992] 1998. *Observations on Modernity.* Stanford, CA: Stanford University Press.

———. 2002. *Theories of Distinction.* Stanford, CA: Stanford University Press.

Lyotard, J-F. 1988. *The Differend.* Minneapolis: University of Minnesota Press.

MacKenzie, D. 2003. "An Equation and Its Worlds: Bricolage, Exemplars, Disunity and Performativity in Economics." *Social Studies of Science* 33 (6): 831–68.

———. 2004. "The Big, Bad Wolf and the Rational Market: Portfolio Insurance, the 1987 Crash and the Performativity of Economics." *Economy and Society* 33 (3): 303–34.

———. 2006. *An Engine, Not a Camera: How Financial Models Shape Markets.* Cambridge: MIT Press.

———. 2007. "The Material Production of Virtuality: Innovation, Cultural Geography and Facticity in Derivatives Markets." *Economy and Society* 35 (3): 355–76.

MacKenzie, D., and Y. Millo. 2001. *Negotiating a Market, Performing Theory: The Historical Sociology of a Financial Derivatives Exchange.* Available at SSRN. http://ssrn.com/abstract=279029 or doi:10.2139/ssrn.279029.

MacKenzie, D., F. Muniesa, and L. Siu, eds. 2007. *Do Economists Make Markets? On Performativity of Economics.* Princeton, NJ: Princeton University Press.

Martin, R. 2002. *Financialization of Daily Life*. Philadelphia: Temple University Press.

———. 2007. *An Empire of Indifference: American War and the Financial Logic of Risk*. Durham, NC: Duke University Press.

———. 2009. "Whose Crisis Is That? Thinking Finance Otherwise." *Ephemera* 9 (4): 344–49.

———. 2010a. "The Good, The Bad, and The Ugly: Economies of Parable." *Cultural Studies* 24 (3): 418–30.

———. 2010b. "Specters of Finance: Limits of Knowledge and the Politics of Crisis." *Journal of Communication Inquiry* 34 (4): 355–65.

Martin, R., M. Rafferty, and D. Bryan. 2008. "Financialization, Risk and Labor." *Competition and Change* 12 (2): 120–32.

Massumi, B., ed. 2002. *A Shock to Thought: Expression after Deleuze and Guattari*. London: Routledge.

Mastnak, T. 2009. *Hobbes' Behemoth: Religion and Democracy*. Exeter, UK: Imprint Academic.

Masur, G. 1973. "Crisis in History." In *Dictionary of the History of Ideas*, edited by P. Wiener, 1: 589–96. New York: Scribners.

Masuzawa, T. 2005. *The Invention of World Religions: or, How European Universalism Was Preserved in the Language of Pluralism*. Chicago: University of Chicago Press.

Maurer, B. 1999. "Forget Locke? From Proprietor to Risk-Bearer in New Logics of Finance." *Public Culture* 11 (2): 47–67.

———. 2003. *Mutual Life, Ltd. Islamic Banking, Alternative Currencies, Lateral Reason*. Princeton, NJ: Princeton University Press.

———. 2005. "Does Money Matter? Abstraction and Substitution in Alternative Financial Forms." In *Materiality*, edited by D. Miller, 140–64. Durham, NC: Duke University Press.

———. 2006a. "The Anthropology of Money." *Annual Review of Anthropology* 35: 15–36.

———. 2006b. *Pious Property. Islamic Mortgages in the United States*. New York: Russell Sage Foundation.

———. 2008. "Resocializing Finance? Or Dressing it in Mufti?" *Journal of Cultural Economy* 1 (1): 65–78.

May, J., and N. Thrift, eds. 2001. *Timespace: Geographies of Temporality*. London: Routledge.

Mbembe, A., and J. Roitman. 1995. "Figures of the Subject in Times of Crisis." *Public Culture* 7: 323–52.

McDonald, L. 2009. *A Colossal Failure of Common Sense: The Inside Story of the Collapse of Lehman Brothers*. New York: Random House.

McLean, B., and J. Nocera. 2010. *All the Devils Are Here: The Hidden History of the Financial Crisis*. New York: Portfolio/Penguin.

Megill, A. 1985. *Prophets of Extremity*. Berkeley: University of California Press.

———. 2007. *Historical Knowledge, Historical Error*. Chicago: University of Chicago Press.

Mehrling, P. 2011. *The New Lombard Street: How the Fed Became the Dealer of Last Resort*. Princeton, NJ: Princeton University Press.

Meillassoux, Q. 2008. *After Finitude: An Essay on the Necessity of Contingency*. New York: Continuum.

Miller, P. 2008. "Calculating Economic Life." *Journal of Cultural Economy* 1 (1): 51–64.

Miller, P., and C. Napier. 1993. "Genealogies of Calculation." *Accounting, Organizations and Society* 18 (7–8): 631–47.

Miller, P., and N. Rose. 2008. *Governing the Present: Administering Economic, Social and Personal Life*. Malden, MA: Polity Press.

Millo, Y., and D. MacKenzie. 2007. "Building a Boundary Object: The Evolution of Financial Risk Management." Centre for Analysis of Risk and Regulation, Discussion Paper 48.

Miyazaki, H., and A. Riles. 2005. "Failure as an Endpoint." In *Global Assemblages: Technology, Politics, and Ethics as Anthropological Problems*, edited by A. Ong and S. Collier, 320–31. Malden, MA: Blackwell.

Moeller, H. 2006. *Luhmann Explained: From Souls to Systems*. Chicago: Open Court Publishing.

Morris, C. 2008. *The Two Trillion Dollar Meltdown: Easy Money, High Rollers, and the Great Credit Crash*. New York: Perseus Books.

Mudge, S. L. 2008. "What Is Neo-liberalism?" *Socio-Economic Review* 6 (4): 703–31.

Mufti, A. 2004. "Critical Secularism: A Reintroduction for Perilous Times." *boundary 2* 31 (2): 1–9.

Münchau, W. 2008. "This Is Not Merely a Subprime Crisis." *Financial Times*, January 14, p. 11.

Muniesa, F. 2007. "Market Technologies and the Pragmatics of Prices." *Economy and Society* 36 (3): 377–95.

Munn, N. 1986. *The Fame of Gawa: A Symbolic Study of Value Transformation in Massim (Papua New Guinea) Society*. Durham, NC: Duke University Press.

Munz, P. 1977. *The Shapes of Time: A New Look at the Philosophy of History*. Middleton, CT: Wesleyan University Press.

Nowotny, H. 2005. *Time: The Modern and Postmodern Experience*. Cambridge: Polity Press.

Nuzzo, A. 2006. "Science, History and Philosophy in Kant and Hegel." In *History, Historicity and Science*, edited by T. Rockmore and J. Margolis, 77–94. Burlington, VT: Ashgate.

O'Connor, J. 1998. *Natural Causes. Essays in Ecological Marxism*. New York: Guilford Press.

O'Malley, P. 2004. *Risk, Uncertainty and Government*. London: Glass House Press.

Orléans, A., ed. 1994. *Analyse économique des conventions*. Paris: Presses Universitaires de France.

Ortiz, H. 2011. "Anthropology—of the Financial Crisis." In *A Handbook of Economic Anthropology*, 2nd ed., edited by J. Carrier, 585–96. Cheltenham: Edward Elgar Publishing.

Osborne, P. 1995. *The Politics of Time: Modernity and Avant-Garde*. New York: Verso.

———. 2010. "A Sudden Topicality: Marx, Nietzsche and the Politics of Crisis." *Radical Philosophy* 160 (March/April): 19–26.

Palan, R. 2006. *The Offshore World: Sovereign Markets, Virtual Places, and Nomad Millionaires*. Ithaca, NY: Cornell University Press.

Palonen, K. 1999. "Rhetorical and Temporal Perspectives on Conceptual Change. Theses on Quentin Skinner and Reinhart Koselleck." *Finnish Yearbook of Political Thought* 3: 41–59.

Palti, E. J. 2010. "From Ideas to Concepts to Metaphors: The German Tradition of Intellectual History and the Complex Fabric of Language." *History and Theory* 49: 194–211.

Parrochia, D. 2008. *La Forme des Crises: Logique et épistémologie*. Seyssel, France: Éditions Champ Vallon.

Parry, J., and M. Bloch, eds. 1989. *Money and the Morality of Exchange*. New York: Cambridge University Press.

Peebles, G. 2010. "The Anthropology of Credit and Debt." *Annual Review of Anthropology* 39: 255–40.

Poon, M. 2009. "From New Deal Institutions to Capital Markets." *Accounting, Organizations and Society* 34: 654–74.

———. 2010. "Systemic Risk in Consumer Finance," *Limn* 1, accessed July 2011, http://limn.it/systemic-risk-in-consumer-finance.

———. 2012. *What Lenders See. A History of the Fair Isaac Scorecard*. Unpublished doctoral dissertation, Department of Sociology, University of California, San Diego.

Poon, M., and R. Wosnitzer. 2012. "Review Essay: Liquidating Corporate America: How Financial Leverage Has Changed the Fundamental Nature of What Is Valuable." *Journal of Cultural Economy* 5 (2): 247–55.

Porter, T. 1986. *The Rise of Statistical Thinking 1820–1900*. Princeton, NJ: Princeton University Press.

———. 1995. *Trust in Numbers: The Pursuit of Objectivity in Science and Public Life*. Princeton, NJ: Princeton University Press.

Power, M. 2007. *Organized Uncertainty: Designing a World of Risk Management*. New York: Oxford University Press.

Pozsar, Z., et al. 2010. "Shadow Banking." Federal Reserve Bank of New York Staff Report 458.

Pryke, M., and J. Allen. 2000. "Monetized Time-Space: Derivatives—Money's 'New Imaginary'?" *Economy and Society* 29 (2): 264–84.

Pryke, M., and P. du Gay. 2007. "Take an Issue: Cultural Economy and Finance." *Economy and Society* 36 (3): 339–54.

Putnam, H. 1995. *Pragmatism.* Oxford: Blackwell.

———. 2002. *The Collapse of the Fact/Value Dichotomy and Other Essays.* Cambridge, MA: Harvard University Press.

Quine, W. V. 1966. *The Ways of Paradox.* Cambridge, MA: Harvard University Press.

Rabb, T. 1975. *The Struggle for Stability in Early Modern Europe.* Oxford: Oxford University Press.

Rabinow, P. 1999. *French DNA. Trouble in Purgatory.* Chicago: University of Chicago Press.

———. 2003. *Anthropos Today.* Princeton, NJ: Princeton University Press.

———. 2008. *Marking Time: On the Anthropology of the Contemporary.* Princeton, NJ: Princeton University Press.

Rabinow, P., G. Marcus, J. Faubion, and T. Rees. 2008. *Designs for an Anthropology of the Contemporary.* Durham, NC: Duke University Press.

Rasch. W. 2000. *Niklas Luhmann's Modernity.* Stanford, CA: Stanford University Press.

———. 2002. Introduction to N. Luhmann, *Theories of Distinction.* Stanford, CA: Stanford University Press.

———. 2012. "Luhmann's Ontology." *Revue international de philosophie* 259: 85–104.

Raz-Krakotzkin, A. 2007. *Exil et souveraineté: Judaisme, sionisme et pensée binationale.* Paris; La Fabrique.

Reddy, S. 1996. "Claims to Expert Knowledge and the Subversion of Democracy: The Triumph of Risk over Uncertainty." *Economy and Society* 25 (2): 222–54.

Redfield, P. 2005. "Doctors, Borders and Life in Crisis." *Cultural Anthropology* 20 (3): 328–61.

———. 2006. "A Less Modest Witness: Collective Advocacy and Motivated Truth in a Medical Humanitarian Movement." *American Ethnologist* 33 (1): 3–26.

———. 2010. "The Verge of Crisis: Doctors without Borders in Uganda." In *Contemporary States of Emergency: The Politics of Military and Humanitarian Interventions,* edited by D. Fassin and M. Pandolfi, 173–95. New York: Zone Books.

Reinhart, C. M., and K. Rogoff. 2009. *This Time Is Different: Eight Centuries of Financial Folly.* Princeton, NJ: Princeton University Press.

Richter, M. 1990. "Reconstructing the History of Political Languages: Pocock, Skinner, and the Geschichtliche Grundbegriffe." *History and Theory* 29 (1): 38–70.

Riles, A. 2011. *Collateral Knowledge: Legal Reasoning in the Global Financial Markets.* Chicago: University of Chicago Press.

Rockmore, T., and J. Margolis, eds. 2006. *History, Historicity and Science.* Burlington, VT: Ashgate.

Roitman, J. 2003. "Unsanctioned Wealth; or, The Productivity of Debt in Northern Cameroon." *Public Culture* 15 (2): 211–37.

———. 2005. *Fiscal Disobedience.* Princeton, NJ: Princeton University Press.

———. Forthcoming. "Africa, Otherwise." In *African Futures,* edited by B. Goldstone, J. Obarrio, and C. Piot. Chicago: University of Chicago Press.

Rorty, R. 1979. *Philosophy and the Mirror of Nature.* Princeton, NJ: Princeton University Press.

Rose, N. 1999. *Governing the Soul: The Shaping of the Private Self.* Cambridge: Cambridge University Press.

Roubini, N., and S. Mihm. 2010. *Crisis Economics: A Crash Course in the Future of Finance.* New York: Penguin.

Said, E. 1979. *Orientalism.* New York: Vintage Books.

Schmitt, C. 1918. "Die Buribunken." *Summa* 1 (4): 89–106.

———. [1922] 1985. *Political Theology: Four Chapters on the Concept of Sovereignty.* Chicago: University of Chicago Press.

Scholes, M. 2009. "The Future of the Derivatives Marketplace." Conference presentation, Derivatives 2009: Looking towards the Future. NASDAQ OMX Derivatives Research Project, Stern School of Business, New York University, November 6.

Shank, J. B. 2008. "Crisis: A Useful Category of Post-Social Scientific Analysis?" *American Historical Review* 113 (4): 1090–99.

Shiller, R. 2008. *The Subprime Solution: How Today's Global Financial Crisis Happened, and What to Do about It?* Princeton, NJ: Princeton University Press.

Skidelsky, R. 2009. *Keynes: The Return of the Master.* New York: Public Affairs.

Smith, D., and S. Tombs. 2000. "Of Course It's Safe, Trust Me! Conceptualising Issues of Risk Management within the 'Risk Society.'" In *Risk Management and Society,* edited by E. Coles, D. Smith, and S. Tombs, 1–30. Dordrecht, the Netherlands: Kluwer Academic Publishers.

Smith, Y. 2010. *ECONned: How Unenlightened Self Interest Undermined Democracy and Corrupted Capitalism.* New York: Palgrave.

Somers, M. 2005. "Let Them Eat Social Capital: Socializing the Market versus Marketizing the Social." *Thesis Eleven* 81 (1): 5–19.

———. 2008. *Genealogies of Citizenship: Markets, Statelessness, and the Right to Have Rights.* Cambridge: Cambridge University Press.

Sorkin, A. 2009. *Too Big to Fail.* New York: Penguin.

Soros, G. 2009. *The Crash of 2008 and What It Means: The New Paradigm for Financial Markets.* New York: PublicAffairs.

Starn, R. 1971. "Historians and 'Crisis.'" *Past and Present* 52: 3–22.

Starr, C., R. Rudman, and C. Whipple. 1976. "Philosophical Basis for Risk Analysis," *Annual Review of Energy* 1: 629–62.

Steinmetz, G. 2003. "The State of Emergency and the Revival of American Imperialism: Toward an Authoritarian Post-Fordism." *Public Culture* 13 (2): 323–45.

Stiglitz, J. 2010. *Freefall: America, Free Markets, and the Sinking of the World Economy.* New York: W. W. Norton.

Strathern, M. 1988. *The Gender of the Gift.* Berkeley: University of California Press.

———. 1992. "Qualified Value: The Perspective of Gift Exchange." In *Barter, Exchange, and Value: An Anthropological Approach,* edited by C. Humphrey and S. Hugh-Jones, 169–91. Cambridge: Cambridge University Press.

Suttles, W. 1968. "To Make My Name Good: A Reexamination of the Southern Kwakiutl Potlatch." *American Anthropologist* 70 (5): 1004–6.

Taleb, N. 2007. *The Black Swan: The Impact of the Highly Improbable.* New York: Random House.

Taussig, M. 1992. *The Nervous System.* New York: Routledge.

———. 1993. *Mimesis and Alterity: A Particular History of the Senses.* London: Routledge.

Tett, G. 2009. *Fool's Gold: The Bold Dream of a Small Tribe at J.P. Morgan Was Corrupted by Wall Street Greed and Unleashed a Catastrophe.* New York: Free Press.

Thomas, N. 1991. *Entangled Objects: Exchange, Material Culture, and Colonialism in the Pacific.* Cambridge, MA: Harvard University Press.

Thrift, N. 2008. *Non-Representational Theory.* London: Routledge.

Touraine, A. 2010. *Après la crise.* Paris: Seuil.

Tribe, K. 1989. "The *Geschichtliche Grundbegriffe* Project: From History of Ideas to Conceptual History. A Review Article." *Comparative Studies in Society and History* 31 (1): 180–84.

———. 2004. "Introduction." In *Futures Past: On the Semantics of Historical Time,* edited by R. Koselleck, vii–xx. New York: Columbia University Press.

Turner, G. 2008. *The Credit Crunch: Housing Bubbles, Globalisation and the Worldwide Economic Crisis.* Ann Arbor, MI: Pluto Press.

Verdery K. 2003. *The Vanishing Hectare: Property and Value in Postsocialist Transylvania.* Ithaca, NY: Cornell University Press.

Verdery, K., and C. Humphrey, eds. 2004. *Property in Question: Value Transformation in the Global Economy.* Oxford: Berg.

Vigh, H. 2008. "Crisis and Chronicity: Anthropological Perspectives on Continuous Conflict and Decline." *Ethnos* 73 (1): 5–24.

Voltaire. [1752] 2000. *Micromégas.* Paris: Librairie Générale Française.

Voltaire, F. M. Arouet, and G. R. Havens. [1759] 1969. *Candide, ou l'optimisme: Edited with intro. notes, and vocabulary.* New York: Holt, Rinehart.

Wark, M. 2006. GAM3R 7H30RY, Institute for the Future of the Book [(2007) *Gamer Theory*]. Cambridge, MA: Harvard University Press.

Weiner, A. 1992. *Inalienable Possessions: The Paradox of Keeping-While-Giving*. Berkeley: University of California Press.

Wellmer, A. 1993. *The Persistence of Modernity*. Cambridge: MIT Press.

White, H. 1973. *Metahistory*. Baltimore, MD: Johns Hopkins University Press.

———. 1978. *Tropics of Discourse*. Baltimore, MD: Johns Hopkins University Press.

———. 2002. Foreword to R. Koselleck, *The Practice of Conceptual History: Timing History, Spacing Concepts*. Stanford, CA: Stanford University Press.

Wolfman, M., and G. Perez. 2001. *Crisis on Infinite Earths*, Absolute edition. DC Comics.

Zuckerman, G. 2009. *The Greatest Trade Ever: The Behind-the-Scenes Story of How John Paulson Defied Wall Street and Made Financial History*. New York: Random House.

INDEX

Africa, 98n6, 114n76
Agamben, Giorgio, 70
Americans for Fairness in Lending, 68
Anthropology, practice of, 98n8
Anti-crisis, 10, 92
Archimedean point of observation, 32
Aristotle, 29, 101n6; Aristotelian legal language, 17
ARMS (adjustable rate mortgages), 61–63
Arrighi, Giovanni, 45
Assemblages, socio-technical, 61, 76–77
Assets, 43, 48–49, 52; market, 72; toxic, 11, 81

Bayle, Pierre, 27
Beck, Ulrich, 75
Begriffsgeschichte, 16
Bernanke, Ben, 83
Big Short, The (Lewis), 50
Brenner, Robert, 45
Bubblistas, 55, 118n24
Butler, Judith, 33–34, 99n15, 110n55

Calculative agencies, 76–78, 94, 124n12, 125n13
Calculative possibilities, 79–81

Callon, Michel, 124n13
Capital: accumulation of, 47, 73; fictious, 46; markets, 43, 46–49, 57–58, 63, 72, 82
Capitalism, 33, 43, 58, 69, 73, 93, 94, 120n39; capitalist expansion, 89; capitalist production, 82; capitalist world system, 43, 46
Capitalization, 82–83
Capitalizing on Crisis (Krippner), 82
Capital Markets Subcommittee, United States, 83
CDOS, 51–52, 55–56, 116n13
Change, 35, 64, 87; historical, 20, 69, 70; social, 23, 106n29
Christianity, narratives of witnessing, 2. See also Witnessing
Christian theology, 17–18, 20, 28, 121n46
Clinton administration, 126n26
Collateral, 46–49, 52, 56, 59
Collateralized debt obligations (CDOs), 51–52, 55–56, 116n13
Commensuration, 60, 64
Congress, United States, 83
Contingency, 9, 32, 35, 38, 85–89, 93–94, 99n14, 114n1, 127n29, 130n6

Contrarians, 53
Control-by-risk, 78–80
Cournot, Augustin, 88
Credit, 11, 46, 48, 58, 61, 72–73, 79–82
Credit default swaps, 51, 53
Credit risk, 77–80
Credit scoring, U.S. consumer, 53–54, 77–80. *See also* FICO scores
Crisis, the, 23
Crisis: accession to, 6, 12, 46–49, 56, 68–69, 72, 83; as a blind spot, 11, 14, 94; and causality, 11, 72–73; and change, 22, 35; concept of, 4–5, 7–8, 10, 16–19, 21, 25, 65–66, 120n39; condition of, 2, 16, 127n30; and critique, 22, 31; as a diagnostic, 4, 7, 9; etymology of, 15; and history, 1, 20, 30; and knowledge, 12–13, 41, 70, 86–87; and narrative forms, 3, 8, 10, 20, 34, 36, 66, 85, 121n45; new times of, 84; and observation, 38–39; and post-structuralist thought, 34; as revelatory, 35, 88–89; as signifier, 9, 19, 29, 36, 59, 64, 82, 93, 101n6; stakes of, 85; temporalization of, 17
Crisis narratives, 41, 49, 85; causality and, 42; in finance, 43, 48, 63–64; production of meaning through, 69–70, 94; social science usage of, 2–3, 7, 11, 36, 41, 67, 71, 85–86, 95, 102n13, 125n14
Crisis of 2007–2009, 5, 10, 41–48, 55, 65, 72
Critique, 26, 28, 99n15; concept of, 29, 35; and contingency, 36; and crisis, 8, 12–13, 22, 35–36, 41, 84, 90, 95, 121n46; and critical theory, 8, 30–33, 67; Enlightenment style of, 23; and judgment, 34; validity of, 31
Critique and Crisis (Koselleck), 106n31

Davis, Kathleen, 30, 103n19
Debt: as asset, 12, 49, 53, 80, 94; manufacture of, 45–55; market, 43, 72,

118n23, 122n4; transformation of, 11, 48, 55–56, 81
Default, 44–45, 48, 50–53, 62–63, 80
Deleuze, Gilles, 95
Deregulation, 49, 58, 82
Derivative logic, 60, 61
Derivatives, 60, 61
Derrida, Jacques, 95
Devaluation, 49, 81–82
Discursive formations, 58, 61, 74

Eco, Umberto, 96
"Economic, the," 69
Economists, liberal, 46, 73, 125n13
Economy: collapse of, 83; as "disembedded," 57; as "real," 43, 58; teleos of, 47
Enlightenment, 24, 30, 105n25; crisis of, 29; politics, 26; rationalists, 31
Epistemic subjects, 37, 112n70
Epistemology, 35, 96; crisis of, 34, 64–69, 113n73
Events, 3, 16, 19, 31, 34, 59, 85–93, 127n29
Expert knowledge, 5–6, 52

Failure: ethical, 9, 14, 31, 94; of knowledge, 63–64, 74; and the market, 12, 53, 62, 72–73, 94; rejection of, 43, 50, 71, 89, 92
Fannie Mae, 78–79
Federal Reserve, United States, 83
FICO scores, 54, 77–79
Finance, 47, 58; constituted by assemblages, 72, 76–77. *See also* Risk
Financial bubble, 4, 47, 55, 59, 73
Financial crisis, 5, 10, 42–43, 50, 93–94; alternatives to, 49; and liquidity, 43, 48, 115n4
Financial devices, 49, 55, 59–62, 76–77, 124n13
Financial governance, 57
Financialization, 57, 82, 84, 86; of life, 56, 61

Financial models, 48–49, 59, 63, 65, 72
Financial practices, 75
Financial products, creation of, 53, 78
First-order observation, 11–12, 37, 49, 99n14
First World War, 31
Foreclosure, 6, 44, 47–48, 67–68
Foucault, Michel, 33, 99n15
Frankfurt School, 32
Freddie Mac, 78–79
French Revolution, 29
Future, 34, 70, 89, 96, 102n14; historical, 16–18, 21, 27–29, 92; uncertainty and, 22, 62–64

Giddens, Anthony, 75
Glass-Steagall Act, 53
Global financial governance, 57
God, 2, 9, 17, 20, 26, 91, 94
Government-sponsored enterprises (GSES), 79
Great Separation, The, 23

Habermas, Jürgen, 32–33, 82
Harvey, David, 44–46, 73, 84
Hegel, G. W. F., 29, 36; Hegelian philosophy, 88
Hippocratic school, 15, 17
Historical consciousness, 7–8, 16–19, 22–25, 29, 31, 104n20
Historical significance, 9, 13–14, 21, 31, 66, 69, 71, 89, 92, 94, 96
Historical transformation, 27–28, 69–70, 73, 84–85
History: and causality, 88, 92; concept of, 16–17, 20, 120n39; and crisis, 3, 7–11, 18, 29, 59, 64, 66, 69, 85, 87; and judgment, 11, 21–22, 27, 31–33, 47, 56; meaning in, 89, 92; and narrative, 4, 24, 95; production of, 13; progress, 42; and reason, 32; signifying, 9, 93; temporalization of, 7, 18–19, 21, 28, 30, 65, 96. See also Secular history
Hobbes, Thomas, 25–26, 107n36

Homeowners, 44, 48, 65–68, 83
Housing bubble, 59. See also Financial bubble
Housing market, 44–45, 49, 55–56, 59
Housing prices, 44–55, 62
Humanitarianism, 121n46
Husserl, Edmund, 111n61

I Have a Dream (King), 1, 96
Inauguration speech, 1–2, 24, 42
Institute for Social Research, 32

Judeo-Christian eschatological framework, 101n9, 128n1
Judgment, 22, 38, 65, 121n46; and crisis, 4, 7–8, 10, 12, 15–16, 41–42, 48, 55, 63, 68–70, 89–90, 101n6; and critique, 29, 32–33; and law, 26–27; and morality, 92–93; truth, 13; and value, 56, 81, 94
Judicium, 17

Kanjorski, Paul, 83
Kant, Immanuel, 19, 28, 33; Kantian critique, 34; Kantian transcendental subject, 37
Keynes, John Maynard, 43
King, Martin Luther, Jr., 1, 6, 96, 97n1
Knight, Frank, 74–75; Knightian uncertainty, 74, 123n6
Knowledge, 10–11, 29, 36–39, 41; crisis as object of, 3–4, 49, 69–70, 86–87, 90; effective and failed forms of, 55, 63–64; limits of, 8, 34, 99n15; production of, 12–13, 66–68, 74–76; proof of, 65
Koselleck, Reinhart, 7, 18–20; and conceptual history, 7–8, 16–17, 25, 69, 101n7; on critique and crisis, 22, 29–31, 121n46; and modern history, 28–29, 103n19; on morality and politics, 23–25, 92; and premodern history, 102n11
Krinô, 15
Krippner, Greta, 58, 82–84

Krisis, 17
Krugman, Paul, 50

Last Judgment, 17–18, 21, 101n11
Lewis, Michael, 50–55
Liberal economists, 46, 73
Liquidity, 43, 48, 59, 72, 78
Locke, John, 26
Löwith, Karl, 104n20
Luhmann, Niklas, 9, 37–38, 99n11,
  99n14, 112n69–71, 113n73

"Market, the," 94
Market creation, 48, 57
Market deregulation, 58
Market devices, 58, 63, 76–78
Martin, Randy, 83
Marx, Karl, 29, 36; Marxist analysis, 43,
  73; Marxist crisis theory, 120n39; Marx-
  ist history of capital, 45
Marxist accounts, 43, 47, 63, 82, 92–93.
  See also Neo-Marxism
Masonic lodges, 24, 27, 92
Material formations, 58–59, 60–61
Material practices, 52–55, 76–77, 94
Maurer, Bill, 52
Middle Ages, 24, 103n19
Modernity, 24, 30, 35, 99n11, 103n19,
  122n48; crisis of, 33, 60–61, 119n33
Money market accounts, 83
Moody's, 54
Morality, 23–28, 92, 105n27, 107n36,
  121n46; and critique, 23, 30–31, 93; and
  knowledge, 29, 108n43
Moral law, 25–26
Moral progress, 26–27
Moral society, 23
Mortgages, 45–48, 80; adjustable rate,
  61–63; subprime, 41, 48–53

Narration, 10, 34, 36, 66, 121n45; and
  contingency, 85; historical, 25, 31; noncrisis, 13; of transition, 24; and writing,
  95. See also Crisis narratives

Narrative forms, 3, 13, 47, 85, 95, 129n5
Narratives, alternative, 13, 50, 68, 71, 75,
  81, 90
National Association of Consumer Advo-
  cates, 68
Natural Law, 23
Natural law, 25–27
Neo-Keynesian, 43, 45–46, 72–73
Neoliberalism, crisis of, 56; neoliberal
  subject, 65, 67, 69
Neo-Marxism, 46, 72–73
Neuzeit, 16–17, 25, 102n14
New Testament, 17
Noncrisis, 12–13, 38, 71
Normativity, 3, 7, 33–35, 66–67, 85

Obama, Barack, 1, 2, 4, 6, 24, 39, 42,
  93, 96
Observation, 38, 39, 99n14, 100n17,
  112n71, 128n1, 130n6. See also First-
  order observation; Second-order obser-
  vation
Occupy movements, global, 84
Occupy Wall Street, 12, 68–69, 83–84
Organized Uncertainty (Power), 74
Orientalism, 103n15, 104n19
Orientalist divide, 24
Otherwise, 9, 32, 92, 98n6, 114n76

Paradox of crisis, 10, 36–39, 81, 94
Parrochia, Daniel, 85–89
Paulson, John, 53
Perfectio, 102n14
Performativity, 76–77, 124n13
Periodization, 20, 24, 29–30, 102n13,
  103n19, 106n28
"Political, the," 69
Political transformation, 24, 69, 96
Politics, 12, 22–26, 30, 35, 87, 92, 96,
  105n27, 107n36, 121n46
Poon, Martha, 53–54, 57, 63, 71, 77–80
Power, Michael, 74–76, 123n9–10
Price, 46, 50; models of, 54, 61–63,
  118n22; naturalization of, 44, 48

Prognosis, 4, 9, 17–18, 21–22, 28, 100n4
Progress, 17, 20, 27–29, 31, 42, 103n18, 108n43
Prophecy, 4, 18, 21

Rabinow, Paul, 6, 95, 98n8
Reason, 36, 94; and contingency, 32; failure of, 74; and judgment, 27, 29–30; limits of, 34; and rationality, 87–88
Recapitalization, 58, 81–82
Reflexivity, 67, 91
Regulation, 52–53, 57–58, 82, 126n20. *See also* Deregulation
Republic of Letters, 24, 27
Revolution, 109n46
Riles, Annelise, 52
Risk: calculation of, 62–63, 74, 77–79; and crisis, 73; as financial product, 52, 55, 80, 126n20; as form of value, 75, 81, as a market, 51, 53; pricing of, 54, 61, 72, 118n22; production of, 75–76, 123n8, 123n10
Risk, Uncertainty, and Profit (Knight), 74
Risk management systems, 75, 79, 81
Risk society, 122n1, 124n10
Roubini, Nouriel, 81

Schiller's dictum, 21–22
Second-order observation, 10, 12, 38, 49, 99n14
Secular history, 2, 23
Secularization, 20, 104n20, 106n28
Secular knowledge, 49, 93, 103n15
Secular modernity, 24
Securities, 44, 80; asset-backed, 52; mortgage-backed, 43–44, 79
Securitization, 52–53, 63, 79
September 11, 2001, 127n30
Shiller, Robert, 45
"Social, the," 57
Social change, 23, 106n29
Social movements, 84, 92
Social science narratives, 2–3, 7, 11, 36, 41, 67, 71, 85–86, 95, 102n13, 125n14

Standard and Poor's, 54
Standardization, 53, 75–76
Starn, Randolph, 85
State of emergency, 127nn30–31
Subject formation, 34–35, 110n57
Subjectivity, crisis of, 65, 67, 69, 113n73
Subprime mortgage market, 57, 61–62, 93–94; constitution of, 77–79
Subprime mortgages, 41, 48–49, 51–53
Superman, 96
Systemic risk, 71–73

Taussig, Michael, 15
Taxpayers, 55–56, 65, 68, 81
Temporality, 7–8, 20, 24, 28, 60, 102n13
Time: and events, 86; historical, 16, 22, 66, 109n49, 113n73; and history, 18–19, 20, 28, 30, 96; prognosis of, 17
Truth, 3–4, 30, 34, 36–37, 81, 92–93; contingency of, 18, 35, 65, 67

Uncertainty, 62–64, 73–75, 87. *See also* Knight, Frank: Knightian uncertainty
United States Federal Reserve, 83
Utopianism, 7, 17, 24–25, 27, 29, 106n31, 109n46

Valuation, 50, 54–55, 65, 76–80, 94, 117n20; claims to errors in, 12, 72; crisis of, 59–60. *See also* Devaluation
Value: calculation of, 72; in debt, 53; erroneous, 46; production of, 50–54, 63, 78; real, 61; in risk, 75, 81; transformation of, 48–49, 94; "true," 55–56, 59, 81–82
Volatility, 72

Wall Street, 53–55
Wealth, generation of, 50, 54–55, 126n20
Western intellectual history, 23
Witnessing, 2, 39, 70, 91, 93, 96, 121n45–46, 128n1